hello life!

First published in 2015
by HEADLINE PUBLISHING GROUP

1

Cataloguing in Publication Data is available from the British Library

Hardback ISBN 978 1 4722 3007 2
Trade Paperback ISBN 978 1 4722 3026 3

Designed by Lynne Eve (design-jam.co.uk)
Photography by Laurie Fletcher (lauriefletcher.com)

Page 61 © Dinodia Photos/Getty Images
Page 100 © Steve Granitz/WireImage
Page 147 © Clemens Bilan/Getty Images
Page 209 © Stroud/Express/Getty Images
Page 213 © Andrew H. Walker/Getty Images

Typeset in Lato and Economica by Google Fonts

Printed and bound in (country) by (printer line)

HEADLINE PUBLISHING GROUP
An Hachette UK Company
Carmelite House
50 Victoria Embankment
London EC4 0DZ

www.headline.co.uk
www.hachette.co.uk

MARCUS BUTLER

with Matt Allen

headline

A NOTE FROM THE AUTHOR This book and the advice it contains is based on my personal experiences of growing up, dealing with the emotional roller coasters of relationships and family, and striving to live a fit, healthy and happy lifestyle. I am not a nutritionist, personal trainer or counsellor. Before following any diet you should consult your doctor as what works for me as a man in his twenties may not be suitable for everyone reading this book. If you are not used to working out, before starting a new fitness routine you should: a) seek medical advice if needed before starting, b) take things at a steady pace and remember not to do more advanced exercises until you are ready, c) cease all exercise and consult a doctor if you feel at all unwell. If you are under sixteen you should consult your parents before making any changes to your diet, exercise routine or lifestyle. And please look after yourself. As you'll see I've done some pretty crazy things in the cause of vlogging. Don't try them at home!

☰ CONTENTS

Intro   6

PART 1: Healthy living   10

PART 2: The dating game   74

PART 3: Friends & family crisis survival guide   120

PART 4: How to get the life you want   186

Conclusion   251

Acknowledgements   254

INTRO

Hello!

And welcome to *Hello Life!*, my guide to being an almost-adult – an indispensable handbook on how not to screw up your future. For some of you, my voluminous quiff and specs might already be a familiar sight from my YouTube channel. You'll know all about my vlogs and online randomness from the internet. For others, I might be an entirely new – and baffling – thing. In which case, you're probably thinking, *Who the hell is this dude? And why has my mum/aunt/gran got me this book?* Good question. How about I give you the answers?

Well, for starters, I'm a vlogger – someone who video-blogs online. Every week or so I upload a new video during which I'll chat about something that's been playing on my mind. Some of this stuff is entirely off the wall. I might moan about the random things that annoyed me during a recent shopping trip, or I'll take the mickey out of my mum and how she drives me crazy sometimes (sorry, Mum).

But there's plenty of serious stuff, too, and having set up my YouTube channel a few years back, I've come into contact with lots of different beautiful, brilliant subscribers (millions of them, in fact). I've shared my experiences with them – both the ups and downs – and believe me, I've gone through plenty of downs, like parental divorce, bullying and bereavement. Through chatting to other people online, I've learned that loads of people my age have gone through the same things. Some of them are struggling as we speak, unsure of how to cope with the problems in their lives. Often my viewers tell me about their problems and, because I've experienced some of the same things, I've been able to deliver some

helpful advice. This happened enough times that in the end I figured,
Hey, wouldn't it be good if I put all this stuff down in a proper book?

I also had something of a life-changing experience recently – a lightning bolt that changed the way I viewed my health for ever. I got fit and I upgraded my diet. I went from being a greedy junk-food-loving couch potato (albeit a new potato, rather than an over-sized baking spud) into someone more health-conscious. By changing my food intake and upping my exercise a little, I became so much happier. I looked better as well.

It struck me that the changes I'd made were easy, I never saw them written about online, or in magazines. Sure, there's plenty of info out there on how to follow the latest fad diet. There are a lot of adverts for expensive gym memberships, too. But nobody was explaining the basics of food, exercise and healthy living. With a lot of research, I came up with a plan that I'm going share with you in these pages, and it won't cost you much, or require you to break your back on a treadmill every day (unless you really want to).

I don't have the final word on the issues of health, dating, family and work stuff – nobody does. What I do have is a lot of experience for a twenty-something in all of those areas, and plenty of useful tips and life hacks that I've picked up along the way. All of them have come from my own successes and failures. Through them, I can hopefully help to make a better you, with a few laughs thrown in, too.

Happy reading!
Marcus

PART 1

HEALTHY LIVING

LIVE RIGHT, LIVE WELL

We'd all like to be healthy, right? All of us want to eat well and feel great, to think sharp and be a hundred per cent happy with the way we are 24/7. For some people that mindset comes naturally. For others, it can seem like an impossible dream that can only be achieved through unhealthy fad diets or back-breaking exercise, both of which are incredibly bad for you.

The reality of living a healthy lifestyle is quite the opposite, and with a few tweaks to your shopping list (or the shopping list of your parents), plus some sensible exercise, it's easy to take control of your well-being. OK, so I know that this might sound like a bold claim coming from some random guy on the internet, but stay with me because I know a few things: I've upgraded my own lifestyle simply by making some sensible dietary changes here and there, while doing a little extra physical activity in the process. Those upgrades have changed me for the better. Now I can help you to make that change, too.

And why would I do that? Well, I'm the generous sort. But also, like a lot of people, I've learned tonnes recently about just how important it is to eat healthily without going on a crash diet. I've also previously been a victim of the advertising campaigns that constantly urge us to gobble up

Naked summer burger with sweet potato, guacamole, salad leaves and tomatoes

crappy fast foods, sweets, alcohol and fizzy drinks. I used to binge and put on weight. It was a bad way to live my life and I don't want to go back to it.

Once I realised what the chocolate and pizzas were doing to me – both mentally and physically – I worked towards a happy and healthy lifestyle by rethinking my eating habits. The changes I made weren't short-term fixes, but long-term solutions. They improved the way I live. They were

Slurping away on my drink in Orlando

affordable, too. These changes didn't involve any revolutionary shopping bills or expensive gym memberships. Instead I made a few sacrifices on the junk-food front, while implementing some tasty alternatives and learning a few training routines in the park.

Before we go on, I'd like to point out that I'm not a nutritionist or a personal trainer. I'd also like to say that I'm not one of those pushy converts to an expensive and painful diet craze – I don't want you to lose weight or make yourself ill in an attempt to get thin. I want you to feel good about yourself, and what I'm going to reveal over the coming pages are the achievable techniques that I've used to improve my life, the ones that turned me into a happier, healthier person. But first, I want to tell you *why* I decided to make a change...

MY JOURNEY

When I was a kid, I was very sporty. I'd often drive my parents crazy, getting them to take me to all sorts of out-of-school activities. I'd be at judo one night and football training the next. I'd play loads of sports at school, including basketball, which I competed at to a high level. I later became a champ gymnast. I loved exercising; I loved winning and I really loved being part of a team.

Over the years, though, I lost interest. By the time I'd got to college, I had given up on pretty much everything and I only played basketball every now and

My first Judo lesson

One of my first gymnastic medals

then. I sometimes went to the gym, but my training was half-hearted and unfocused. Worse, I ate terribly. Crisps, fizzy drinks, chocolate, cheese and takeaway burgers were my five a day, and I was so naive when it came to the basics of diet and nutrition that I convinced myself that I was eating healthily just because I had a bit of lettuce in my sandwich.

Me drinking a Coke on holiday

It got worse. A couple of years ago, before YouTube had really taken off, I worked full-time at an estate agent. During that period I was living off the worst food in the world. I'd eat three packets of crisps every day without even thinking about it. I became addicted to diet soda and I'd use food for comfort. If ever I was feeling down I'd eat chocolate. When I was hungry I'd gobble up whatever sugary foods I could get my hands on. I had no idea that the crap going into my body was causing a vicious cycle of cravings, all of them tricking my brain into thinking it needed to consume more and more unhealthy foods.

I'd always been a slim kid, but I was getting a bit lumpy around the edges. I wasn't obese, but when I looked in the mirror I was becoming unhappy with what I saw. There was a time when I was trim and fit; suddenly I was a little bit overweight – you could call it puppy fat, I guess (or just fat) – and I wanted to look good and feel healthier. My only problem was that I didn't know how to get there. I had no idea about dieting, and a lot of the things I was reading in fitness magazines or on health websites seemed unachievable – and a little scary.

In the end, I spoke to my younger sister, Heidi, because she used to work in a gym (she's currently a footballer in America, so she knows her stuff). She put me in touch with a personal trainer called Jermayne, who got me to talk about what it was I really wanted to achieve realistically. I guess that was the first step. People often go into their gym with unrealistic goals, like 'I want to have a body like Scarlett Johansson.' Jermayne got me to settle on an achievable target, which was to look better and to feel better. And we all want that, right?

'How serious are you about getting into this, Marcus?' he said. 'Because we can just exercise to make you feel better, or you can really go for it. And if you're gonna get really in shape we'll need our work to be more of a lifestyle transformation.'

I decided to go for it. I set a goal to change my life, not just in the amount of exercise I did every week, but also in the way I lived through food and drink. I became fascinated with the science behind diet. I'd ask a million

Jermayne Williams –
my trainer and friend who
helped inspire my healthy
lifestyle transition

questions every week, usually on what foods I should eat and what I should drink. I've always been a question-asker. I'm the kind of person who loves to listen to advice and other people's stories. I'm like a sponge; I'll soak everything up and then I'll make my decisions based on what I've learned.

'IT WAS THE DIET FIZZY DRINKS I WAS ADDICTED TO. THEY CAN CAUSE A PERSON TO CRAVE EVEN MORE SUGAR.'

Luckily Jermayne was full of information. When he got into the nuts and bolts of my diet, he could quickly see why I had been struggling – it was the diet fizzy drinks I was addicted to. He told me they can cause a person to crave even more sugar. 'They're the catalyst for diet disasters,' he said.

I went home and researched what seemed like a pretty bold statement. But there it was: pages and pages of personal recollections from people saying how their cravings for sugar had ended once they'd said farewell to the diet drinks. In the end I swapped cans of fizzy drink and junk food for healthy smoothies and balanced meals made up of good proteins like chicken and fish, plus vegetables, including spinach and sweet potato.

If you're thinking, *Er, yeah, whatever, Marcus. That food is pretty rank.* Well, that's what I thought at first, but I was surprised at just how tasty it became once I got into cooking it. Jermayne told me the difference between good carbs (wholegrains and oats, sweet potatoes) and not so good (white bread and pasta, white potatoes); I dropped sugary cereal and took to porridge instead. Once I'd upgraded my diet, I then started to notice the changes in my body. I was slimming down. My cravings started to vanish.

After around six months, I'd lost three stone in body fat just from changing the foods I was eating and exercising more. My skin was better. I had way more energy and fewer mood swings. I felt more positive, and that's because I was happier with how I looked and felt.

The 'crashes' disappeared, too. By that I mean the slumps that always seemed to come around an hour or so after a chocolate bar or fizzy drink. Back in the day those sugary products were giving me an instant hit – a rush – and I would think, *Whoa! I feel good!*. But not long afterwards I'd be burned out, tired and my body would crave another hit of sugar. By changing up my diet, I was able to create a consistent and comfortable energy level. Sure, I'd still get tired, but overall I was more energetic and more productive – because I was eating and drinking the right stuff.

A while after changing my lifestyle, I started to look better. I wasn't skinny – I didn't want to be – but I had sharp edges around my muscles, and I wasn't even going to the gym. I was working out in the park every other day, running and doing push-ups, crunches and tricep dips off benches. I even used a 'free bar' at the park to work on my pull-up game. (To begin with, I struggled to complete one rep.)

People were starting to notice. I'd get compliments on how I looked, and not just about my physique. Friends commented on my healthy glow. It was clear to everyone that my life had changed, and for the better, so I told anyone who asked, 'Look, it wasn't that hard. Anyone can do it.' Some of them took my advice on board and are reaping the benefits today. Now I'm going to tell you exactly what I told them...

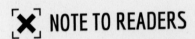 **NOTE TO READERS**

Everything I'm going recommend to you in the coming pages is affordable. I know not everyone can splash out on a gym membership or personal trainer, so all the exercises and activities here are free (you can do them anywhere, and might only need a park bench as a piece of equipment) and the foods that you might want to consider introducing to your diet won't make too much of a dent in your finances.

Getting those gains!

EVERYTHING IN MODERATION

One of the biggest things I've learned about adopting a healthy lifestyle is that diet is the most important factor. Sure, exercise is vital, too, but I'd say it's a seventy per cent diet/thirty per cent exercise ratio when it comes to getting the well-being you want. That famous saying about your body being a temple is so true. Think about what you're putting into your tummy. Fill it with goodness and you'll shine. Load it with crap and, chances are, you'll feel crap (after the initial five minutes of pleasure has worn off).

If you want to make a big, big change to your lifestyle, then I seriously recommend you consider reducing the following food and drink in your daily diet – and I use the term 'food and drink' loosely. Fizzy drinks and unhealthy snacks like crisps, junk and super-sugary foods: this stuff is pretty light on nutritional goodness.

When I reduced these food groups in my diet, I know my life changed considerably, both physically and mentally. I felt better. I looked better. I *thought* better. I don't think I could go back to the way I was when I was a junk-loving, fizzy-drink-downing 'food sweeper' (you'll read about that gross habit a bit later). My diet is completely different now, and as a result I'm a changed person. Follow my advice and you can make a huge change to your life, too.

At the same time, it's important that you understand the concept of moderation. A lot of the things I've mentioned in my list aren't going to do you harm if you munch them every now and then. I also know that sometimes it's impossible to eat healthily all the time. I might have a day where I eat a burger and chips and, afterwards, I'll think, *Yeah, that was great. It was nice to remind myself of how good a burger tastes.* I just don't need to eat one every day. I can have a burger every three or four weeks. Likewise, crisps and chocolate. A little every now and then can be a nice treat and, overall, I'd estimate my diet is currently ninety per cent good. But I wasn't always that way, and by considerably reducing the following five food types my life changed for the better. It can change for you as well. Give it a go!

1 ▶ FIZZY DRINKS

Confession time: back in the day, when I didn't care about my diet, I would drink three cans of fizzy drink a day, slugging from a fresh one as if it were a bottle of water, often to rehydrate myself, regardless of the added sugar content and crazy additives. I'd think, *Oh, I'm thirsty. I'm having a drink.* It was rarely for taste reasons. It was always out of necessity rather than a luxury. I was addicted.

After a little research I learned that some fizzy drinks are bad for a number of reasons. The 'full-fat' versions have a huge refined sugar content. When you drink them, your energy levels peak as the sugar goes in. You'll then get really tired – or crash – as those energy levels fall. Before you know it, you're craving another sugary rush to get you up again, which is seriously bad for your health, especially if you start to scoff chocolate and sweets to kill the withdrawals.

A number of diet drinks are just as bad, if not worse. Forget the hype about zero calories because these products are brimming with artificial flavours, chemicals and sweeteners. At times, they may trigger the brain into craving sugary things – more drinks, chocolate, sweets. They can also release insulin into your body, which flicks your metabolism from 'athlete' to 'fat storage' mode.

2 ▸ CRISPS

Before I changed my diet, I'd easily go through three packs of crisps a day without even thinking about it. For lunch, I'd often make a toasted sandwich with melted cheese oozing from the sides, accompanied by two bags of crisps on the plate (different flavours, mixed up). In between meals I'd often snack on crisps and chocolate, all of which meant I was eating a lot of crap and putting on weight.

We all know that crisps are bad for us, but it's easy to get fooled. Sometimes a packet might claim there's only eighty calories per bag, and that sounds great. But there's usually zero nutritional value to those eighty calories. You won't find any vitamins or healthy nutrients in there, and around eighty per cent of the listed ingredients sound like something you'd learn about in a chemistry lesson. Next time, look at the label before you start to snack. It can be pretty off-putting.

I often feel like society is to blame for our obsession with unhealthy snacks. Wherever you turn on the high street, you'll find shops selling chocolate and crisps. I recently watched a show on junk-food-loving kids, which focused on children between the ages of four and sixteen. They were overweight and suffering from crazy health problems. One kid even had eleven teeth taken out because of all the sugary foods he'd been consuming. He was in agony afterwards and it had everything to do with a poor diet.

☒ LIFE HACK!

A quick tip when considering this dietary upgrade: a step-by-step approach works best. Don't change everything in one go. You'll probably go crazy with withdrawals and boredom. Instead, pick one thing and concentrate on reducing it in your diet for three weeks. I guarantee that if you last the distance you won't go back. Then pick another category. And another. Before you know it, you'll be halfway to a healthier you.

Oh, and remember: it's not about the calories, it's about what your food is made of that counts. Two hundred calories of nutritious natural ingredients is better than something carrying ten calories of artificial rubbish.

3 ▶ WHITE BREAD, POTATOES, WHITE PASTA

I used to love white bread, especially sandwiches and toast. But when I was eating white bread, white pasta or potatoes, I was putting refined carbohydrates into my body. Carbs, when they're behaving, give you energy, but if you don't use all of that energy, then it soon turns into fat.

Not all carbs are bad for you, though. You can still eat bread and pasta, but it's much better for you to try them in a wholegrain form. Do that and you'll be better off, because when a carb is complex – in its natural form, with all the nutrients attached, as they are in wholegrain products – it breaks down slowly. When you can, think about replacing these refined carbs with their wholegrain counterparts. As soon as I made this change, I felt my energy levels increase.

4 ▶ ANYTHING WITH HIGH ADDED SUGAR CONTENT

OK, a bit dramatic I know, but if you're looking at the ingredients on a product and the first one is sugar – white sugar especially – then think twice. It's so bad for you – it rots your teeth, it messes with your metabolism and the fructose molecule in sugar is thought to fool the brain into thinking that the body isn't full when it really is. And be careful what you believe when you read the nutritional info on sugary products. So many companies slap a logo on their packet, which reads 'No Added Sugar'. It sounds great, doesn't it? But that doesn't mean there's zero sugar in it. Instead it's just a slightly misleading way of saying there aren't any extra sugars on top of what's already in there.

Don't be fooled by the word natural on a label. Not all products claiming to be natural are good for you. For example, people often eat fruity cereal bars thinking they're healthy, when in reality they may be high in sugar and contain just as many calories as a chocolate bar.

5 ▶ JUNK FOOD

I used to love junk. For a while in my teens I'd eat fast food all the time. Me and my friend Dave went through a phase of being addicted to it. After a night on the town I'd order twenty chicken nuggets with a double cheeseburger, plus fries. I'd down the lot. Pizzas were ordered twice a week. There was even a spell on a lads' holiday to Turkey where I ate so much junk I became mates with the people working behind the counter at the burger van. I have a photo somewhere of me messing around with the staff. I was seventeen and a bit greedy, especially after a couple of beers.

Even worse, I would food-sweep after I'd finished my meal. I'd look at what was going on with my friends' food and eat anything they'd left behind. Then, I would walk around grabbing whatever food had been left behind by randomers, too.

'Don't you want the rest of that burger? OK, I'll have it...'
'Eating those fries? No? I will...'

The basic facts of junk foods are this: they carry a huge fat content, they're nearly always fried, and can contain high levels of sugar. All of these things are bad for you. In fact, there's nothing good in junk food. And the only thing you'll gain from eating too much of it is a lot of weight and a short-lived sense of satisfaction.

'TAKE CARE
OF YOUR BODY.
IT'S THE ONLY
PLACE YOU
HAVE TO
LIVE IN.'

EAT YOUR WAY TO HAPPINESS

OK, so I've told you the foods you should consider minimising if you want to become healthier. Now I'm going to tell you about the stuff you *should* be eating: complex carbohydrates and lean protein – food that's high in nutritional value, with minerals and vitamins. Basically fruit and veg, plus stuff you can snack on throughout the day, like popcorn, or a handful of nuts, which should stave off those cravings for crisps and cakes.

1 ▶ SWEET POTATO

My personal trainer, Jermayne, first turned me on to sweet potato. He said, 'Look, man, try it with lunch rather than crisps and sandwiches. Put some sweet potato in a salad with chicken. Make some wedges out of it; it's awesome!' I admit it, though, the first time I had it, I thought, *This tastes a little bit strange.* My sister used to have it with her roast dinner and I thought it was weird.

I persevered, and I'm so glad I did. That first week I had a sweet potato for lunch every day and eventually I ended up loving them. Now it's one of my go-to foods and a vital part of my diet because it's a complex carb. That means it breaks down slowly (unlike a refined carb, like normal potatoes or white pasta), giving me energy for longer periods of time. Sweet potato is also extremely high in vitamin B6, which I've heard may help to prevent heart disease, as well as helping with PMS symptoms, depression and skin blemishes. It's seriously good stuff.

It's not just found in sweet potato, though. Other foods that are high in vitamin B6 include sunflower seeds (a great snack), fish like tuna and salmon, turkey and pistachios (though try and keep those nuts plain). If you're unconvinced, give some sweet potato wedges a try. Cook them up in coconut oil and add a little flavour with some cajun spice or smoked paprika. Whack them in the oven with the skin still on for forty minutes – it's super-healthy and so tasty.

2 ▶ BLUEBERRIES

These were a mystery to me back in the day. I might have had them in a muffin, or as part of a dessert every now and then, but I'd never snacked on blueberries before. Now I'm always eating from a packet between meals because they're one of the fruits with the lowest amounts of sugar. They're also packed full of antioxidants – chemicals that seemingly block those nasty 'free radicals', which can make you more at risk of cancer.

Whenever I'm craving something sweet, I tend to turn to blueberries for help. Those urges usually come around nine or ten o'clock at night, a couple of hours after I've eaten dinner. If I eat blueberries I don't have to worry about them keeping me awake because they're low in sugar. They'll kill my hunger without giving me a crazy sugar rush afterwards. I also put them in my cereal and smoothies, and snack on them during the day.

3 ▶ QUINOA

My friends always take the mickey out of me for the amount of quinoa I eat, but it's honestly changed my diet big time. The simple facts of it are this: quinoa is a bit like rice, but the amount of protein per grain is incredibly high,

which is what makes it so healthy. If you're a vegetarian or vegan, it's also a great way of getting some protein into your diet without eating meat.

These days I'll have quinoa with curries; I'll put it in salads instead of rice. It only takes ten or fifteen minutes to boil and you can chop up tomatoes or onions and throw them into the pot to add a little extra flavour. A vegetable or chicken stock cube is a nice addition, too.

4 ▶ ALMOND BUTTER

My mum tried to introduce me to almond butter for six years without any real luck. I was never a peanut butter lover so it seemed a big step for me, but once I got into it I absolutely loved it. Now I'll put it on my rye toast in the mornings, and I snack on it and drop it into my smoothies.

Whenever I travel anywhere I'll always pack a pot of the stuff so I can spread it on some crackers when I'm staying in a hotel. It's a healthy snack that can get me through the day, especially if I'm too busy to cook anything. It's so good. If you don't believe me, check the label: most brands are a hundred per cent crushed almonds and all natural, as well as being high in good fats and protein.

Almond milk is also a great alternative to traditional cows' milk. As humans, our bodies aren't actually made to consume dairy products. A surprising number of people can't digest dairy properly and it leaves them bloated, gassy and tired. I switched to almond milk not so long ago and liked it. Now I use it with cereals, coffee and smoothies, and it's a lot better for you as long as you stick with the unsweetened versions. Sweetened almond milk often contains a lot of sugar.

5 ▶ GREENS

I guess I was lucky, because even when I was young Mum would make dinners that came loaded with vegetables. My snacking habits were bad, but most of my evening meals were served up with tonnes of veg. There was stuff like spinach, kale, greens and broccoli, plus loads of peas. All the stuff you're supposed to eat to maintain a healthy diet. I lapped it up.

It helped that I was a fan of the cartoon *Popeye* when I was a kid. If you haven't seen it, Popeye was a sailor who used to crack open a tin of spinach every time he was in trouble. The greens used to give him super-strength, and I would always think, *What's so good about that stuff?* It was only when I researched the benefits of spinach recently that I discovered just how high it is in protein for a veg. So it's true what they say, then: if you want to grow up big and strong, eat your greens. Seriously, they're important.

6 ▶ FISH

Fish is a great way to get good proteins into your diet, and tuna, salmon and cod are all very high in protein. Oily fish also contains a lot of omega-3, which is important because it may help lower the risk of heart disease, depression, dementia and arthritis.

Still unconvinced? Well, here's a little biology for you: a lot of shellfish contain iron, which is stored in your liver, spleen and bone marrow and helps develop red blood cells. These carry oxygen around your body. Without them your cells would become starved of oxygen, your brain and muscles wouldn't function properly, and your immune system might become a bit sketchy. And that's just the start of the problems, so get some iron in your diet! (Oh, and lean meats are also great for this like chicken, turkey and lean beef.)

It's taken me a while to get there, though. I used to hate that unmistakable fishy taste until about a year ago when I started to try things like sea bass. That eventually got me on to things like salmon (but only very recently) and these days I can cook a bloody good tuna steak – that's my fave. But I'm so glad fish is a part of my diet now.

7 ▶ RYE BREAD

If you want a healthier alternative to a doorstep-cut, white loaf, try rye bread. My mum has always been really into this. She'd eat it with almond butter and I couldn't understand the fuss at first. But I've recently got into it and it's so nice! It can be even healthier than many wholewheat breads. If I'm in a rush of a morning, I'll toast some and add a little almond butter. Delicious.

Make sure to look at the ingredients when you buy rye bread, though. Some brands still contain a lot of refined sugars, so always check for whole rye flour and other natural ingredients. Another thing to look out for on food labels is the phrase 'Low GI'. This refers to the glycaemic index – a measurement of a carbohydrate's impact on a person's blood glucose levels. If that sounds too scientific, just remember that, in general, low GI is good, high GI is bad.

8 ▶ SPARKLING WATER

Cutting out diet drinks was a huge step for me because it killed a lot of the cravings I had for other unhealthy foods. In the end I got over my addiction

by adding freshly squeezed limes or lemon to sparkling water. OK, I know it sounds boring, but once you're used to it, it's great. And so much better than tooth rot.

9 ▶ DARK CHOCOLATE

Milk chocolate is so moreish. I used to open a pack with the idea of eating a chunk or two, and before I knew it, I'd have wolfed down the whole block. Dark

chocolate is tasty – so tasty once you get used to it – but it's bitter, especially if you're eating a type that's around seventy per cent cocoa content (which I'd recommend), so it's much harder to eat more than a couple of squares in one hit.

The transition is hard at first, but once you're there I guarantee you it's even harder to go back. I've eaten milk chocolate recently and thought, *Wow, that's too sweet!* Dark chocolate, like blueberries, is also high in antioxidants, which are so vital in battling those unpleasant free radicals, and it's great for killing a sweet craving.

10 ▶ POPCORN

A healthier alternative to crisps and amazing when sprinkled with rock salt (not drowned in toffee), air-popped popcorn only contains 31 calories per cup. It's a wholegrain, which is good for your diet, plus it contains complex carbs. It's also naturally low in calories and fat. So get stuck in!

THE SMOOTHIE &
JUICE MASTERCLASS

I love smoothies. They're full of flavour and goodness, and they're easy to make. Load them up with vegetables and add some fruit for a sweet hit, and you'll soon find that these concoctions make a refreshing alternative to concentrated fruit juices or fizzy drinks. They're also an easy way to consume a load of nutrients in one hit.

Think about it. In your lunch you might eat chicken, quinoa and one portion of kale. But in a smoothie you can whack a lot of different vegetables in at once – albeit in smaller portions – which means you can access loads more nutrients, though they shouldn't replace all your meals.

It took me a while to get used to them, though. My personal trainer first suggested I try smoothies and, I admit it, the first one tasted disgusting. It was full of green veg and it came out sludgy. I took one sip and spat it out.

'Ugh, that is rank!' I shouted. 'How can anyone drink that?'

My mum was in the kitchen at the time. She took a sip and liked it, though she was used to eating healthier foods than me, plus I still had a sweet tooth. She suggested that I add a bit more fruit just to give it some flavour and eventually I got used to the taste and the texture. Now I love them.

Coming up with your own recipes is fun, too. If you find a blend and can think of something that might make it taste even better, just add it next time. I've listed some of my favourite mixes for you to try, so just chuck the ingredients in and blitz away!

① GREEN JUICE

- Two large handfuls of spinach
- Two large handfuls of kale
- Two celery sticks
- Juice of one lemon, freshly squeezed
- A hint of ginger

② CHOCOLATE SMOOTHIE

- Two bananas (better frozen)
- One and a half tablespoons of raw cacao powder
- One tablespoon of cacao nibs
- One tablespoon of almond butter
- One cup of almond milk

③ BREAKFAST SMOOTHIE

- Handful of spinach
- One banana
- A third of a cup of oats
- One tablespoon of almond butter
- One tablespoon of flaxseed
- A handful of berries (strawberries, blueberries or raspberries)
- A splash of coconut water (or normal water if you prefer)

④ THE ENERGY BOMB JUICE

- Four carrots
- Two cubes of ginger
- One apple

One & four are both better if made with a cold-press machine, but it's still possible to make a great juice in a blender.

I CAN REBUILD YOU

I'll never forget my first personal training session. After an initial meeting with Jermayne, we decided to have our first workout at the local park. He asked me to run a lap of the grounds, which was probably around two kilometres, but I couldn't do it. Halfway round I had to stop. I was out of breath, sweating and feeling a little bit sick.

This isn't cool, I thought. *I used to travel the country playing basketball and doing gymnastics. Now I can't even run a kilometre. What's going on?*

Actually, that's a lie. What I was really thinking was, *Makeitstop! Makeitstop! Aaaaaagh!*

Through the sweat and the tears, Jermayne could tell I was frustrated with my performance. After a while he worked out a basic programme for me to stick to, and once I got into it I could see the results quite quickly. I looked better. I felt better. I had more energy, and my moods were always up. The physical activity released loads of endorphins – the feel-good chemicals in your brain that give you an 'exercise high' every time you work hard physically. I'd always loved sports as a kid, and with Jermayne I was doing something that I really enjoyed. I looked forward to every session. Well, most sessions.

I found that being active is great, not just for your health and your state of mind, but also your social life too because when it comes to workouts you don't have to exercise solo like me. You might want to train with some friends.

Maybe team sports are more your thing, in which case why not join a netball or football team? Try out some different sports until you hit upon one that suits you. You'll discover that getting sweaty in the fresh air is the first step to a new improved lifestyle.

THE GYM-FREE WORKOUT

If you don't want to invest in a gym membership or you're self-conscious about exercising in front of other people, there are plenty of things you can do at home to get started. For example, who needs the gym when you've got circuit training? If you haven't heard of this before, circuit training is a body-conditioning routine, which relies on aerobics or strength building. You basically complete a load of exercises on a 'circuit' (hence the name) and it's one of the more hard-core ways to get your body into shape. The intensity is super-high and the exercises are really tough, but because you don't need any equipment for a lot of the drills, it's an easy thing to do wherever you are in the world. These drills can take place in your bedroom, living room or outside in the garden. (I've found it's always nice to work out in a little rain.)

The routine I've listed here will make you feel hot, sweaty, maybe even sick, and the first few sessions will be the worst, but you'll start getting fitter as you go. After a few weeks you'll feel stronger. Set yourself realistic goals, though. If you've never done a push-up in your life don't go for ten reps on your first try – you'll blow a muscle. Instead, run through the circuit gently and see what level you're at, and do a suitable number of reps for each. Write down your limits and use them as a motivation to push yourself forwards. Try to improve the reps with every week. Also, make sure you warm up beforehand – this is always vital before any exercise activity. You can mix up thirty seconds of star jumps with thirty seconds of running, thirty seconds of butt kicks (where you run on the spot, kicking your legs up, so your heels bang against your backside) and thirty seconds of high knees (again running on the spot, but with your knees high in the air). Complete this twice and your heart rate will go up. Then stretch a few important muscle groups – hamstrings, calves, groin – to prevent injury.

OK, got your trainers on? Then on your marks... get set... GO!

1 ▶ Burpees (10 reps if you can)

OK, to do these, you'll need to start in a standing position. Drop to the floor in the squat position with your hands on the ground then, in a quick movement, kick both feet back so your legs are extended out, as if you were about to do a push-up. To complete the move, return your legs to the squat position, before jumping up.

2 ▶ Tricep dips (10 reps)

These can be done on a chair, park bench or from the end of your bed. Sit on the edge, with your palms holding the surface. Then, straightening your arms, push up and lower your bum down so it's nearly resting on the ground – repeat this in an up-and-down motion. Slower is harder.

3 ▶ Squats (10 reps)

Stand with your legs shoulder-width apart. With your arms stretched in front of you for balance, drop down into the squatting position and then slowly push back up again. Remember to keep your back straight at all times and not to let your knees roll forwards past your toes.

4 ▶ Press-ups
(10 reps if you can)

Getting sweaty and super-achy? Then use your knees for support, especially if you're struggling to complete the reps. There are also plenty of advanced techniques for the fitter ones among you. Look up Spider-Man press-ups, diamond press-ups and one-hand-extending press-ups. These are all things to work towards, but you won't thank me for them the next day. Your body is going to feel some serious pain!

5 ▶ Mountain climbers (30-45 seconds)

It's like real-life mountain climbing. Stand on the spot and lift your one knee really high in a running motion. At the same time, reach for the sky with your opposite arm. Repeat on the other side. Imagine you are pulling yourself up a mountain. It's tough!

6 ▶ Plank (30 seconds)

Adopt the push-up position, but rest your weight on your elbows and forearms, keeping your elbows directly underneath your shoulders. With a straight back, push up on to your toes so your body is in a straight line. You'll feel your abs tightening. Hold this pose for thirty seconds.

Feeling like a super-hero? Then move on to the dreaded plank leg raise: take the same position, but lift your right foot off the ground and hold for a second before returning to the start position. Repeat with your left and keep alternating. Uh-oh! Here comes the burn!

7 ▶ Lunges (20 of these, please)

Ten forward walking lunges and ten backward walking lunges. Begin by standing with your back straight but relaxed, and point your chin up. Maintaining your balance, step forwards with your right leg, then lower your hips until both knees are bent to around the ninety-degree angle. Your front knee should be directly above the ankle; don't touch the floor with your other knee. Push up and move forwards straight on to the next leg. When you've completed ten, slowly repeat the same process, but backwards. This is the hard bit!

8 ▶ Bicycle crunches (30 seconds)

Do these for thirty seconds and unleash your inner Bradley Wiggins (but, please, not your inner Lance Armstrong). Lie on your back with your knees bent, feet on the floor. Put your hands behind your head. Push your lower back into the floor (though a mat might be nicer) then raise your upper back, shoulders and head up, tightening your tummy muscles as you move. At the same time, bring your right elbow and left knee together while straightening your right leg (don't let it touch the ground), in a similar motion to pushing the pedals on a bike.

That's just the first part! Next, bring your right knee back up. Move your left elbow and right knee towards each other while straightening your left leg; that's just one rep – you need to do a few more, so get pedalling. It sounds complicated at first, but once you get into the swing of it you'll soon feel the benefit.

9 ▶ Leg raises (10 reps if you can)

Lie on your back, with your arms by your side, palms down on the ground.
Lift your legs – ankles and feet together – at a forty-five-degree angle. Then
straighten, or raise your legs to a ninety-degree angle so they're in line with
your hips. Lower again to a forty-five-degree angle. These are great for your
core, the muscles that run through the middle of your body, like your abs (or
six-pack).

Try ten reps. This exercise
can be made harder
simply by lowering your
legs at a slower rate – try
descending your legs
for three seconds, then
raising them for three.

10 ▶ Split lunge jumps (10 reps)

These are similar to squats, but much more of a mish. Copy the starting position, but rather than pushing forwards, so you're standing straight, push up and jump, moving your legs in a scissor motion, so you land in a reverse lunge position. Come on! You've got ten reps in you!

Now take a minute's breather, and go again. Aim to do this circuit two to four times in a session, and go for it up to four days a week if you can. Be sure to have a day's rest between sessions so your body can fully recover. You won't believe the transformation. Well, that's if you stick to a healthy-eating plan.

CALLING MR ASS-KICKER

You need to do a home workout, but you're struggling for motivation? Here's some 'can-do' activities to set you on your way...

1 ▶ MAKE YOUR GOALS VISUAL

When I first started to shape my body, I found a 'body role model' to give me inspiration, someone I wanted to look like. In my case, I chose the actor Zac Efron because he was lean and looked in good shape. I had a bit of a man crush on him. (Who doesn't?). I downloaded a picture of him to my phone, though not as my actual screen saver because that would be a bit weird, and whenever I felt lethargic before a session I used his picture as inspiration. PS: these days I've upgraded to Ryan Reynolds. Sorry, Zac!

2 ▶ TAKE BODY-EVOLUTION PICTURES AT HOME

When I started working out, one of my goals was to look better. I didn't like what I was seeing in the mirror, so Jermayne told me to take a body-evolution picture of myself every week. (I've still got them all.) That way I could watch my fitness and body evolving, and now I use these pictures to push myself. If ever I'm feeling lazy, I'll scroll to the first ones and think, *I don't want to go back to that.*

BODY EVOLUTION :-)

3 ▶ SET REALISTIC GOALS

So you want to look like Brad Pitt in *Fight Club*? Of course you do. But you will need an amazing personal trainer, a hard-core gym regime and diet, plus the willpower to do it. All of these things cost serious cash. If you're at college, school or in a full-time job, you probably won't have the time either, so set realistic goals instead, like losing a couple of notches on the belt. Take a photo, hit that target and then move on to the next one. You'll quickly see progress and you'll feel encouraged. Set an unrealistic goal (you want legs like Taylor Swift's, say) and it's easy to become disheartened, especially if you fail to see immediate results.

4 ▶ THE MOTIVATIONAL PLAYLIST

Everyone has a song that can inspire them, one that can push them to their physical limits. Thing is, those songs can become boring with repeated plays. I use an app called 8tracks that has playlists for every mood. Now my gym sessions are soundtracked by random high-tempo tunes. (You can pick the genre you want, too.) Even better, they sometimes drop samples from famous speeches to push you even harder. It really helps on the treadmill when you've got Arnie Schwarzenegger in your ear telling you to 'Work hard-errrrr!'

5 ▶ SEE YOUR SUCCESSES IN ADVANCE

I played basketball for Sussex and Brighton Bears Juniors when I was younger. Our coach was into psychological training, and before games he would play clips of great professional teams, like the Chicago Bulls. He would then show us crazy documentaries on their successes. He'd tell us, 'Picture in your head how you're going to play – that pass you're gonna make, or that shot you're gonna hit.' It made me believe in myself. So when it comes to your training, get a boost by imagining yourself running for twenty minutes without stopping beforehand, or maxing out your reps on the weight machine... Then go for it!

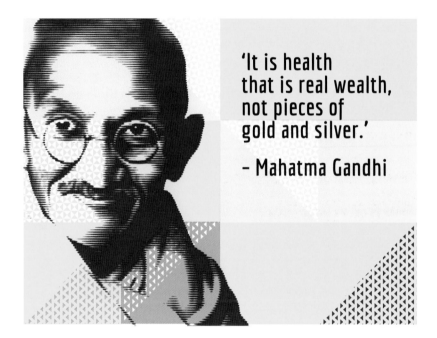

'It is health that is real wealth, not pieces of gold and silver.'

– Mahatma Gandhi

'NO MATTER HOW SLOW
YOU'RE RUNNING,
YOU'RE LAPPING
EVERYONE SITTING ON
THE SOFA.'

WHAT NOT TO DO AT THE GYM

If you do decide the gym's the place for you (and why wouldn't you? It's a great place to get fit), then there are some golden rules you should live by. Because working out should be the only reason you're there...

1 ▶ DON'T SHOW OFF

If you're on the running machine for the first time in weeks, don't set it to level twenty, 'just to see what happens'. I went with Dad once and he pushed his speed up too high, lost his balance and flew off the back of the treadmill. He ended up smacking his face on the floor. Fair play, he got back up and carried on. I would have left red-faced, never to return.

2 ▶ DON'T BIG YOURSELF UP

Why try to impress a room full of randomers by lifting loads of weights? I always see people at the chest bar, their arms collapsing under overloaded weights, body pinned to the bench, wailing for help – 'Aaaaargh!' Don't be that person. It's not big and it's not clever.

3 ▶ NO GYM SELFIES

OK, I admit it: I've done this before. But on my one and only occasion of extreme vanity, I immediately thought, *What am I doing with my life?* The gym is not the place to stand in front of a mirror, top off, flexing your biceps. People can see you Instagramming your chest, and it looks ridiculous. Especially if you're waving a selfie stick around.

4 ▶ DON'T SCREAM

Grunting I understand. Sometimes I need that extra ten per cent, so a little 'Grrrrr!' can push me to the finishing line. Just don't finish your set with a Godzilla-style roar, or throw your weights to the floor with a loud crash. Do what you want to do, but don't involve the whole gym because you'll look like a bit of a knob. Keep the sex noises to the bedroom.

5 ▶ NO ONE LIKES THE DRIP

I'm a sweater, but I make sure to never leave my drip on the machines. Not everyone thinks the same way, though, and it's gross. The other day

Posey gym selfie. Don't get caught doing this.

I got on an exercise bike and the handlebars were shining with sweat. The seat was drenched, too. I nearly vommed. Please clean up!

6 ▶ CHATTING PEOPLE UP IN THE GYM

You're beetroot-red, sweaty and stinky. What part of that combination could possibly seem attractive to a perfectly normal member of society? Well, unless you're both into that sweaty look… then by all means, knock yourself out.

HOW TO GET A GOOD NIGHT'S SLEEP

OK, here are some things you probably didn't know about sleep. One, it's just as important to your well-being as diet or exercise. Two, people who don't get enough rest often feel their hunger levels increasing – that's because their leptin levels drop (the hormone that regulates appetite), and so the munchies kick in. And, three, humans are the only mammals that deliberately fight off the zeds.

But a good night's rest is sometimes hard to come by. We've all been there: the evening before that important exam, driving test or crucial work presentation. For some reason the brain just won't quit, despite those heavy eyelids. So relax. Literally. Here are some tips to guarantee you a peaceful eight hours of recuperation...

1 ▶ NATURAL NOISE IS COOL

The gentle patter of rain, the crashing of tropical waves, some chirruping jungle birds – all of these things can send your brain into snooze mode. Don't worry if you don't live on a tropical island either. Plenty of apps are available to recreate these soothing noises. The ambient samples will also shut out any passing traffic if you play them loudly enough (or through your headphones).

2 ▶ BUT SILENCE IS EVEN BETTER

I can't deal with noises at night, like a clock in the room or a rattling radiator. I remember staying with my YouTube friend, Tyler Oakley, in America. He had a clock that kept tick-tick-ticking all night. I tried to silence the thing, but

I couldn't find the batteries, so in the end I wrapped it up in my clothes and shoved it in a cupboard. He hated me for that, especially as the night before I'd spilled red wine on his cream carpet. I'm not the best of house guests, am I?

3 ▶ RELAX THE BRAIN

If you go to bed straight after a long computer or phone session, your eyes will seem tired, but a million thoughts can zip through your head at once, especially if you've been murdering zombies or zoning out on *Candy Crush*. Give yourself a tech-free hour before you hit the hay.

4 ▶ FEELING BORED WITHOUT YOUR PHONE?

Then read. Books, magazines, amazing self-help guides by YouTubers: all these things can bring calm to your mind.

5 ▶ STAY FROSTY

This might just be me, but hot rooms don't do it for me. If the heating's on, I'm sweating and wide-eyed-awake. I like it best when it's a bit chilly and I can wrap myself in the duvet. Cold pillows are also key, so here's a quick life hack: put pillowcases in your fridge during a heatwave. Take them out before you get to bed, and you'll feel chilled, no matter what the thermometer says.

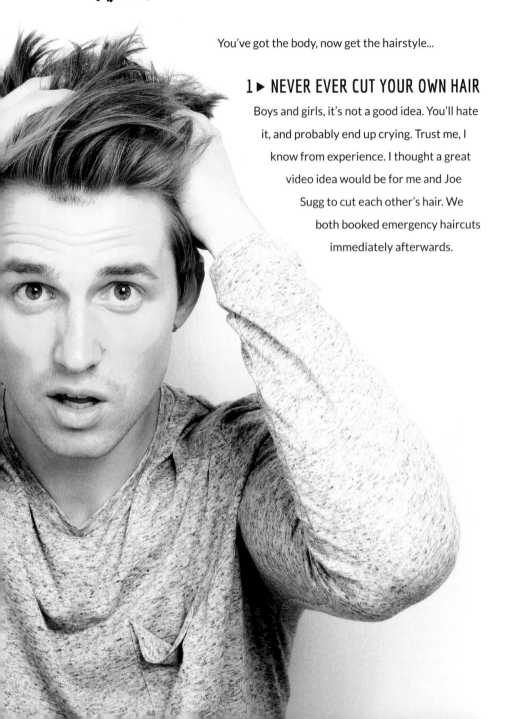

HOW TO AVOID A HAIRCUT DISASTER

You've got the body, now get the hairstyle...

1 ▶ NEVER EVER CUT YOUR OWN HAIR

Boys and girls, it's not a good idea. You'll hate it, and probably end up crying. Trust me, I know from experience. I thought a great video idea would be for me and Joe Sugg to cut each other's hair. We both booked emergency haircuts immediately afterwards.

2 ▶ BE REALISTIC

I've occasionally had ambitious ideas, but they rarely come off. I might look at Harry Styles and think, *Hmm, cool look – I'd like that.* But never in a million years is it going to work on me because my hair is so different.

3 ▶ ALWAYS ASK YOUR HAIRDRESSER

People always say, 'I want something different. I want a change. I want a new me.' But they rarely know what it is they actually want. Your hairdresser is the expert, so trust them. They'll guide you through the process. That's assuming your hairdresser has been trained.

4 ▶ PHOTOS ALWAYS HELP FOR INSPIRATION

Whenever I've wanted to change my hair in the past I'd often take some pictures in to my stylist and say, 'I want something like this – what do you think?' If they couldn't give me exactly what I wanted they'd always point me in the direction of a look that would suit me. Though always refer to point two on this list.

5 ▶ DON'T BE AFRAID OF TRYING SOMETHING NEW

People are getting more cautious about their hair, especially guys. And if you're sitting in the stylist's chair afterwards, thinking, *Oh my god it's a bit short!*, why worry? If you're going for a dramatic redesign, maybe take it slowly at first. Don't go for the rainbow Mohican straight off, start gradually. And remember, it will grow back (hopefully).

BREAKFAST

MY CHOCOLATE PORRIDGE

I like to make this with oats, almond milk, raw cacao powder, almonds, raisins, with blueberries and raspberries on top.

POACHED EGGS WITH SPINACH

On rye bread and almond butter, if you like that.

LUNCH

SWEET POTATO SALAD (VEGAN)

Mixed vegetables (greens like broccoli, spinach, beans, etc.) with sliced roasted sweet potato and quinoa. Drizzled in extra virgin olive oil.

ROASTED VEGETABLES WITH SMOKED PAPRIKA CHICKEN

Best with root vegetables, like carrots, parsnips and sweet potatoes.

DINNER

TUNA STEAK

Tuna steak, with tenderstem broccoli and a hint of lemon.

HANDFUL OF NUTS

SNACKS

FRESH
FRUIT

ALMOND BUTTER
ON RICE CAKES

PART 2

THE DATING GAME

Relationships can be a bit of a weird thing. One minute you're happy, buzzing, in love. The next you're dumped, crying into your pizza and deleting pictures of your ex from Facebook. It feels like someone's slapped you around the face. You can't concentrate; you can't get out of bed. It's just about the worst feeling in the world.

But the highs, when they come along, make it all worthwhile. I should know; I've had a few lows, but now I'm with my long-term girlfriend, Niomi, and all the bumps and moody relationships of the past seem insignificant, though they felt pretty big at the time.

I guess Narcus (as some people call us online) first got started at school, probably in year six. We were both ten, and Niomi was the new girl in the year. At that time I was a bit cheeky – I would often sit at the back of the class and make jokes about her. It was nothing horrible. I just enjoyed teasing Niomi and flirting, basically because when I first saw her my initial reaction was, 'Wow, who's *she*?'

It probably wasn't until year seven, when we were twelve, that we became friends, but for the first couple of years nothing really happened. Our sets in schools got mixed about and we were split up when I started getting into trouble. I had a bit of a bad phase and I'd been influenced by some of the more troublesome kids at school. I was skipping lessons and misbehaving. It was nothing major, but in an attempt to keep me on the straight and narrow, the teachers pulled me into a meeting at the end of the term.

'OK, Marcus, we think you've got real potential,' they said. 'But you're being influenced by the wrong people, so we're going to move you into a class of new kids.'

I wasn't happy. *Great*, I thought. *I'm leaving all my mates, and my classmates, and I'm being put into a group of new people who nobody knows? Brilliant. That's really going to help me out. This is so not cool.*

Niomi and me on our last day of school – aged sixteen

Starting a new year at school is normally exciting. You can't wait to see the mates you left behind before the summer, and you've always got loads of stories to tell about what you've been up to during the holidays. This time around, I was dreading it. I was going back to a new form in year eight, with a new form teacher and loads of people who were fresh from other schools. Some of those kids even knew each other from their previous classes, so they were going to have their own gangs and cliques. I really didn't want to go back to lessons that year.

I'd still see Niomi around, though, and school life changed with year ten and GCSEs. I chose my options and when it came to the first English lesson, Niomi walked into the room. She had been put in my set, and we ended up sitting next to each other. We'd talk every day and mess around. In the end, I started to get a bit of a crush on her.

Looking back, I was a bit of a ladies' man. I loved flirting and I'd started dating different girls at that time, so I probably thought I was great, a real player. Thinking about some of those moments in class – conversations with Niomi – makes me cringe now, though. I was desperately trying to impress her and I was probably making a right idiot of myself while doing it.

But it wasn't a one-way street; Niomi was flirting, too, and one evening at a friend's party we ended up kissing. I was so happy. *This is cool*, I thought. *She's great!* And after that, we started seeing each other, but, man, relationships in the classroom are *weird*.

I should have been prepared for it because I'd been involved in one or two before meeting Niomi. The first happened in year seven with a girl who I won't name, but we were madly in love and we stuck together for around a year, which felt like a long time back then. We genuinely thought we were going to be together for ever, which seems funny now. We were so young. Why would we seriously believe that?

Inevitably we broke up, which felt like the biggest thing in the world (though it wasn't really), and after that there were one or two other girls. But then Niomi came along, though even that was strange at first because the one thing that happens when you start dating someone at school is that you both fall into the 'dating code' trap.

This goes in three phases:

STAGE 1: 'Seeing' one another

STAGE 2: Going steady

STAGE 3: Serious couple,
      aka 'official'

This is the first-ever photo of me and Niomi (which is why it's such rubbish quality!)

Wow, it can be stressful at times. And that's before you even get to the day-to-day discussions about how you should behave in school. For example, do you hold hands at break? I know in my head I wanted to play it cool in front of my mates. I also wanted to play it cool in front of Niomi's, and I guess, for that reason, the relationship never really progressed from the 'seeing' phase to 'official'. After kissing and hanging out for a bit, we became cool friends. I saw other girls, she saw other boys, and it all fizzled out, and I think I was a little bit gutted about it at the time. But that was all to change once the pair of us enrolled at college...

Niomi and I would always hang out together at college. She was in a relationship with some guy, and I was in and out of short romances, but nothing really serious. We'd still always meet up in free periods and after school, and I really liked her. I think she really liked me back then, too.

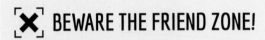 BEWARE THE FRIEND ZONE!

The Friend Zone is a really dangerous place to be when you fancy someone. It's also very easy to stumble into. Basically it's that area where you flirt with someone you fancy so much, and hang out with them so often, that they become a proper friend, rather than a love interest. You like them, you don't know whether they like you, and suddenly asking them out on a date seems super-weird because your relationship is platonic.

Messing it up would also be really painful, so my advice is to stay out of the Friend Zone at all costs. Sure, when you fancy someone be nice to them. Be friendly and flirt. But make your move before you wander into the Friend Zone, because getting out of it is a bit of a mish. And if you blow it, you've lost a friend as well as a potential partner. *Ouch.*

I first realised I was in trouble when we all went out to a club in Brighton. We somehow managed to get in even though we were all seventeen, which seemed so exciting at the time. There were four of us – Niomi and me, my best mate, Max, and one of Niomi's friends. I guess it felt a little double-dateish at the time, but it definitely wasn't. Niomi had an 'official' boyfriend at the time. But after a few drinks I started feeling all these emotions stirring up. I kept talking to her and thinking, *Wow, I wish you were my girlfriend.*

Right there in the club, I remember saying, 'I have feelings for you.' It all got a bit awkward and nothing happened until a few weeks later when we were chatting on Facebook Messenger. I really wanted to explain that I still had all these feelings for her, but I was struggling to find the courage to 'fess up. In the end I just typed it out, and in a pretty blunt way.

> **MARCUS: I don't think you should be with your boyfriend...**
> **NIOMI: What do you mean?**
> **MARCUS: I think I really fancy you. I want to go out with you, like properly, because obviously we had our thing before. I want you to be my girlfriend.**
> **NIOMI: I'm in a relationship and I can't leave him.**
> **MARCUS: ...**

What a downer. Looking back, that really should have been that, but I knew she wasn't happy with her guy, not really. To me, they just didn't seem right as a couple, so when they split up a few months later, I wasn't surprised at all. In fact, I was delighted. *Yes!* I thought. *Now we can do something!*

That moment arrived when we were both at a friend's eighteenth birthday party. We danced. We flirted. We kissed. We haven't looked back since. We made the transition from 'seeing' one another to 'official' like it was the easiest thing in the world, and five years later we're still going strong.

There have been plenty of bumps in the road for Niomi and me, and like all relationships we have to work at it. Moving your way up from 'single' to 'blissfully happy' is a tough road to negotiate, especially when you haven't had that much experience. I learned from my own mistakes when it came to asking people out, likewise dating and then dumping people. I got to understand the hard way about issues such as dealing with heartbreak. And I've also picked up a few tips on how to make a relationship work. I'm going to walk you through all of those subjects in this section. Hopefully you'll be able to make use of it.

I'd like to think that I've got a bit of experience in this area. Just because I'm young, it doesn't mean I don't experience big feelings. All of us will go through love and loss in our young-adult lives, and the emotions and dilemmas are just as challenging for us in our teens and twenties as they are for an older person.

I remember when Niomi and I first started as an 'official' couple, there was some chat about how it was going to work once Niomi started studying at the University of the West of England. We'd already spent some time apart. I was working full time in Brighton, plus I'd been away for a few months backpacking around Australia with Max. When I got back, I'd often spend my weekends seeing her, but it was tough for a while. In my head, I was full of paranoia. Was Niomi going to meet someone cooler than me in the student union bar? Someone nicer than me? Someone better-looking? That fear was constantly going through my mind.

We got through it, though, and now we're stronger than ever. We live together in London and we support one another in our day-to-day lives.

For example, when Niomi left university, having completed her law degree, she wasn't sure what she wanted to do. She was in a position that so many people find themselves in when they graduate. She had spent so much money on her education but she became uncertain, thinking, *What am I doing with my life? Have I chosen the wrong thing? Will I even enjoy a job in law?*

Celebrating Niomi graduating from university in Bristol

At that stage in our relationship, YouTube was starting to become a big thing for me. I was twenty-one-ish, and so was Niomi, and I knew she was into fashion, so I suggested she write a blog.

'Who's going to read it?' she said. 'Trust me, you'd be surprised. You're into food and fashion. You're fashionable. You have your passions and your interests. Talk about that!'

She still wasn't sure, and it was only once we'd been travelling to America together that she decided to go for it. Niomi's a very good writer, so when she was working in a shoe shop while she figured out what she wanted to do for a career, she got her blog off the ground.

I guess it was only natural that she would end up on YouTube. Niomi appeared in my vlogs every now and then. People were making really nice comments, like, 'Oh she's so sweet, she should start her own channel!' In the end Niomi set up her own thing. The fans of her blog followed her over to YouTube and it's been such a success that her channel is now a full-time job for her.

Niomi and me on holiday at Disney in Florida

We're extremely lucky that, because of our jobs, we get to spend lots of time together. We can even go travelling together, to places such as LA. Our lives work. Sure, we bicker about the washing-up and things like that, but we don't argue on the big issues. We've found a great balance in our relationship.

But like I mentioned earlier, getting there hasn't been easy. Love can be a nerve-wracking business, especially when you're trying to work out who you are and what you want to do with your life. Even fancying someone can feel like a burden, especially if you're unable to work through the feelings and hormones that are bombarding your brain. Trust me, I know. I've been there. Hopefully, my notes on this always-complicated subject can help to ease your stress.

FINDING YOURSELF

OK, before we get into the whole dating-game thing, I just want to deal with the issue of sexuality. Love is tough enough without chucking sexual preferences into the mix, especially if you're still figuring out whether to date boys or girls. It can be a scary time for some people. And you might even have to make some tough decisions along the way. But the one thing you must understand as you enter this new chapter in your life is that you *will* find happiness.

It's something I'm passionate about, even though I don't have a coming-out story of my own. And I really don't want to look like I'm trying to give advice on something I haven't experienced myself. Instead, what I have are the recollections from my gay friends – stories from when they came out. All of them have told me that the people who loved them before, loved them exactly the same after they'd revealed their sexuality. They were scared about what their parents and friends would think at first. But what actually happened was that their life choices were accepted. Their families were supportive. They told them, 'What were you scared about? You haven't changed as a person. You're still the same, it's no different, and we still love you.' I know this isn't true for everyone, so the internet can also be a great place to get advice and talk to people about this issue. But we'll come to that in a second.

Making the announcement can be hard, though. But the one thing you have to remember is that **IT'S OK TO BE YOURSELF**. You might not think that way when you're growing up because, as a kid, everything you're fed on the TV and in the movies tells you that you have to meet your prince or princess in a straight romance. There are no gay relationships in any of the Disney films we all watch when we're little. I guess I understand that life was different when those films were made, but even now a lot of romcoms are straight.

When you make the decision, you'll probably find that your announcement will be greeted in one of two ways, and **YOU CAN NEVER PREDICT PEOPLE'S REACTIONS**. I have to admit, from my friends' experiences, I've only heard the positive stuff. Two close mates of mine came out recently and they were so pleased. Their lives changed. It was as if a whole weight, or pressure, had been lifted off their shoulders. They were happy and comfortable in themselves, and they seemed like new people once they had made their announcement.

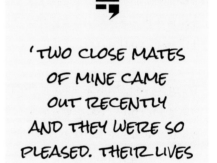

'TWO CLOSE MATES OF MINE CAME OUT RECENTLY AND THEY WERE SO PLEASED. THEIR LIVES CHANGED.'

But I know that this isn't always the case. Some people find it incredibly difficult to communicate with their parents on issues of sexuality. And it might be that, for some members of your family, being gay still seems weird, or wrong. They're from a generation that don't get it, in which case, there could be arguments, disputes and heartbreak at home. If you have no one in your family to turn to, life can become very painful.

Luckily there are people on hand to help you through these tricky times. Vlogs are a great comfort. My friends, the YouTuber Connor Franta, and the Australian actor Troye Sivan, both came out as gay on YouTube. Troye explained how he discovered his sexuality, and the difficulties he experienced in coming out – their videos have loads of reassuring advice in them. My YouTube friend Tyler Oakley supports The Trevor Project, which is an organisation that focuses on preventing suicide in the gay, lesbian, bisexual and transgender (LGBTQ) communities. If you go to *www.thetrevorproject.org* you'll be able to read loads of info on the subject.

There are also plenty of support groups online, such as Being Gay Is Okay – or *www.bgiok.org.uk* – which was designed to help people under the age of twenty-five. Their site has plenty of tips on how to come out to your friends and family, plus lots of useful, life-changing advice. But if you feel you really need to talk to someone straight away, you can contact the London Lesbian and Gay Switchboard who provide confidential support for people throughout the UK. They can be reached at 0300 330 0630 and *www.llgs.org.uk*. They might not be able to calm your mum and dad down at first, but they will be able to help *you*.

The Trevor Project
thetrevorproject.org

Being Gay Is Okay
bgiok.org.uk

London Lesbian
and Gay Switchboard
llgs.org.uk
0300 330 0630

WILL YOU GO OUT WITH ME?

OK, first things first. You fancy someone. This is good news. They're hot, funny, smart, the most gorgeous thing you've ever laid your eyes on and, undoubtedly, without question, The One. The bad news is that now you've got to figure out what to do next. Unless you're telepathic, this Object of Desire is probably unaware of your affections, so here are some pointers that should set you on your way to asking them out on the first of (hopefully) many dates.

1 ▶ BE REALISTIC

Sorry to be a Debbie Downer here, but you need to know your limits in the dating game. Be brutally honest with yourself. If a guy you fancy is usually drawn to the bookish indie-kid type and you're a lithe, smiley beach volleyball hotshot, he might not be interested. Just saying.

2 ▶ BUILD UP THE COURAGE

Confidence is key. When I was at school it was a nightmare asking someone out. The smartphone technology wasn't there for me to flirt with someone I fancied, or deliver the question. I had to do it face to face, or on Messenger after school. Now you can ping someone with your phone and it's sorted in seconds.

But even with that in mind, you still need to build the confidence to engage with a person you're crushing on, because asking them out cold probably isn't going to work. You'll have to build some kind of relationship with them first (though beware the previously discussed Friend Zone!), so chat to them in class, or before a work meeting.

It's important to remember at this stage that subtlety is very important. If you like someone, don't go into the conversation with a desperate mindset, where you're thinking, *I like this person. I have to start a conversation with them!* Your body language might throw them off and your entire game plan will have been busted. Especially if you go up to them with the line: 'Hi, you don't know me, but I think I'm in love with you.' *Cringe.*

3 ▶ DO SOME GROUNDWORK

You've identified The One. You've successfully negotiated Stage Two, so now you have to find out a little more about your Object of Desire. Talk to them. Find out what they're into, whether that's music, fashion, art or sports. If there's some common ground, seize it. Build up a relationship and work out what makes that other person tick.

4 ▶ FLIRT

Don't be scared to flirt. If you're feeling a connection with someone at college or work, drop a subtle hint. Sometimes a smile across the office is enough, or a reassuring joke when things are getting a little bit stressful during revision sessions – that kind of thing. It's always good if you can make someone laugh, and if your jokes are being reciprocated, there's a good chance that this person likes you back. Never, under any circumstances, ever wink at them. *Ugh!*

I know that with Niomi and me, it was a friend thing at first, though we weren't quite in the Friend Zone. I was always telling mates, 'Yeah, I fancy her, but does she fancy me?' I'd flirt with anyone, and I wouldn't mind if they didn't

Never, under any circumstances, ever wink at them

flirt back. I'd just laugh about it. So when Niomi started flirting, too, I thought, *Wow, this is cool!* She wanted to take it forwards as well. Our chemistry helped it to happen.

OK, now it's decision time. If you're feeling uber-confident, skip to Stage Six, otherwise read on...

5 ► TECHNOLOGY IS YOUR FRIEND

Use it. All that stuff is vital in the modern dating game. Writing down your feelings in a text or email gives you time and space. You haven't got to face someone and you can plan what you want to say. It might even be an idea to bounce your message or mail off a friend for advice first. They can tell you whether you sound a bit stalkerish or not.

There is one downside to approaching someone online, and that's the lack of reaction. It's impossible to see how someone is taking your exciting offer of a lunch date in the local coffee shop. Are they jumping for joy, or recoiling in horror? Every possible outcome will flash through your mind as you see the dreaded '...' symbol flashing at the bottom of your text box. Get ready. Death or glory is coming your way...

6 ► TOP-LEVEL DATING S***

So you want to do it the old-school way: through proper chat. Well, congrats. Being able to ask someone out in person is great. It shows courage, and it proves you can speak about your emotions. But it's also advanced stuff. It's the ninja school of dating.

I remember at school, thinking, *I really like this person, and I really like that person, but I'm not going to ask them out.* I'd imagine the worst-case scenario, like asking a girl out and having her laugh in my face. Then her friends laughing in my face. And everyone in school rinsing me for it afterwards. But then I always figured, *What's the worst thing that can happen?* Seriously, if the risk of having someone reject you and laugh at you is all that's getting in the way of your journey to true love, then toughen up.

Always remember the basics, though: clean teeth, have a shower, do your hair. But if the other person is into body odour and dirty fingernails, then by all means don't wash for a week or two.

7 ▶ PREPARE FOR SUCCESS

They've said 'Yes'. Sweet! So now what? Make sure you've got somewhere to suggest straight away. Don't leave the idea of a date hanging because the other person will think you're not that serious. Instead, have something and somewhere in mind, which, if you've nailed Stage Three should come easily.

8 ▶ READY YOURSELF FOR FAILURE

Rejection hurts, I know, and the level of pain will depend on the depth of your feelings. But you will get over it. And it's important that you don't lose your self-belief. When you've been knocked back, it's so easy to go into a negative spiral, to think: *Great, I fancy that person, she doesn't fancy me, so that means that no one else is going to fancy me.* Before long you've gone into free fall. *Am I always going to be on my own? What's wrong with me? What the hell?!*

The truth is, if they've said 'No', think, *Great – one less person to waste my mental calories on.* Concentrate on meeting someone who is interested in you instead, and, believe me, there are plenty of options out there for everyone.

BANISH THOSE FIRST-DATE NERVES FOR EVER

Going on a first date can be a nerve-wracking experience. But with a few nifty life hacks you can quickly settle the butterflies...

1 ▶ LOOK HOT!

Get dressed up in something you know you'll look amazing in (so maybe not a mankini). If you're unsure, snap a pic of you in your outfit and send it to mates for a second opinion.

2 ▶ LOOK CONFIDENT

Stand up straight, and don't slouch at the table. It'll work wonders for your mood. But don't stand up *too* straight when you walk in for the first time. At best you'll seem arrogant, at worst you'll look like a robot.

3 ▶ PREPARE A FEW TALKING POINTS BEFOREHAND...

Not 'What's your favourite colour?' Instead, think of a few things that are going to get your date interested, stuff that you know they're into. Or maybe drop in some interesting subjects, such as:

- What's on your bucket list?
- Craziest thing you've ever done?
- If you could hang out with anyone in the world, who would it be?

Do your prep, because no one likes an awkward silence. They're called 'awkward' for a reason, yeah?

4 ▶ ...BUT REMEMBER: IT'S NOT A JOB INTERVIEW

Because a constant stream of questions is just *weird*.

5 ▶ UNLEASH YOUR INNER LION!

If you're really stressed, nip to the loo, lock yourself in a cubicle and get animal-like: adopt a power pose by standing straight for a minute with your legs wide apart. Place your hands behind your head and then lean back. I know, super-weird, right? But trust me, it'll unleash your inner lion and the confidence will surge through you (some science dudes from an American uni figured this out). Just don't spend too long in there...

6 ▶ THE ME, ME, ME CHECKLIST

Remember the time you scored the winning goal in a cup final, or aced that karaoke competition? Got a special talent? A swimming badge? Look good in skinny jeans? Just before you show up for a first date, run a checklist in your brain of all things you're proud of. Trust me, you'll be buzzing with self-belief afterwards.

7 ▶ YOU'RE NOT THE ONLY ONE...

Take a little comfort in remembering that the person you're meeting has said 'Yes' to hanging out with you. That's a start! Chances are, he or she will be a bit nervous, too. And why not? You're hot stuff!

MOVE YOUR BODY

Want to know how your date is going at a glance? Then check their body language for clues.

YOU'RE IN IF...

- They're playfully fiddling with jewellery or hair.
- Your date is mirroring your body language – it shows they may be interested in you.
- Your date leans in while you're telling the one about how you embarrassingly locked yourself in an aeroplane toilet.
- Their feet are pointing towards you. If those toes are wiggling happily, you might want to think about ordering a taxi back to your place!
- They have uncrossed legs in a comfortable pose. Always a good sign.
- They're in an open-armed pose with upturned palms. They're *so* into you.
- You're receiving longing gazes and smiles, twinned with an occasional shy downward glance. This is a positive sign rather than an indication you've got food stuck to your face.

YOU'RE OUT IF...

- Your date is making space between the two of you while you talk.
- They're pointing their feet away from you.
- They're rubbing their eyes, scratching their nose or massaging the back of their neck. These are heavy hints that your usual charm and chat isn't working.
- There's a strange look or two. You might want to start thinking about your next target.
- Their legs are crossed and their arms folded. Time to get the hell out!

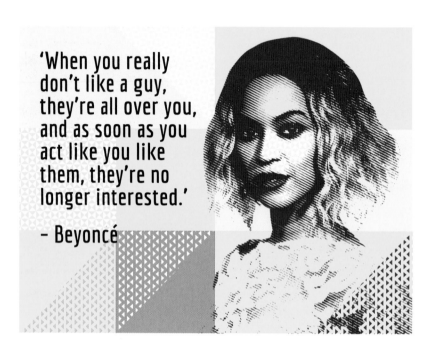

'When you really don't like a guy, they're all over you, and as soon as you act like you like them, they're no longer interested.'

– Beyoncé

THE SOCIAL MEDIA RELATIONSHIP WORKSHOP

As if life wasn't complicated enough, then along came social media. For some of you, it's always been there – a constant source of communication throughout your life, where everyone and everything can be linked with the swipe of a finger. For others, the world changed for ever, seemingly overnight, with the introduction of Facebook, Twitter, Instagram and all the other places where we can hang out online.

All of these sites are great. They can make the world a smaller place, terrifyingly so sometimes. They've connected people who had lost touch a long time ago. I've built an entire career out of it! You can even pull on social media these days (not that I've done it). But there are pitfalls, especially when it comes to a budding romance and relationship issues. Here are the traps everyone should avoid when playing out their love life via the internet.

When I decided to walk home from a bar with virtually no clothes on... First (lads') holiday, aged seventeen

RULE 1 ▶ DITCH THE PICTURES OF YOUR EX

It's easy, after a year or so, to forget about an ex, but it's good to have a spring clean every now and then. Sweep away all those cuddly photos. The minute you meet someone new they will do a little bit of healthy Facebook stalking (we all do it). If there's a new person that you like, do you really want them to see those old pictures of you and your ex?

RULE 2 ▶ DON'T BECOME FRIENDS WITH MUM ON FACEBOOK

She'll see all your terrible photos. She'll see your partner's terrible photos, and you'll both be miserable for ever. Unless your mum's cool, in which case it'll be all right.

RULE 3 ▶ NAKED SELFIES ARE NEVER A GOOD IDEA

Never, ever, *ever*. It's not going to get you anywhere with anyone and you both could get into serious trouble with the police, especially if you start sending them out willy-nilly (excuse the pun). Even if they're for personal use only, there are some seriously dodgy hackers out there. Before you know it, your 'arty filtered naked selfie' could be all over the web.

'BEFORE YOU KNOW IT, YOUR 'ARTY FILTERED NAKED SELFIE' COULD BE ALL OVER THE WEB.'

Here's a little lesson from my college days: there was once this couple who filmed themselves having sex, when all of a sudden the guy's mum walked into the bedroom. There was a bit of a scene, some shouting, clothes were thrown on very quickly. It was all very *American Pie*. Over the next few days, the dude involved showed the video to a few friends. I guess he thought it was funny. The joke was soon on him when the video was texted to a less-trustworthy mate. Before long, everyone in college had seen their racy home movie – and I mean *everyone*.

One day, the poor bloke even came into class only to clock his dangly bits being played on a projector screen (the teacher had yet to come in, I'd like to point out. It wasn't Biology) and he was rinsed for the rest of the year. So think of that story if ever you're tempted to take a naked selfie. Sure, if you want to know what you look like naked have a look in the mirror, but keep it private and never ever take a naked picture to share. Got that?

RULE 4 ▶ DON'T BE A RELATIONSHIP ATTENTION-SEEKER

I see people on the internet who seem to get a kick out of writing their life story online. So your boyfriend has dumped you? OK, pour your heart out to some friends in private. The rest of the world doesn't need to know how awful he was every single day of the week.

Then there are those friends who love to leave a cryptic cliffhanger in a desperate attempt to get some interest from the outside world. Usually it'll go something like this:

> **'Well, I didn't see that coming. FML.'**
> **'I can't believe he did that...'**

Someone will usually take the bait. They'll ask, 'Whassup, babe?' Before they know it, they've been bombarded with a page-long rant about some relationship issue or other. Beware of these people: they're on a fishing exercise. Instead of seeking advice from someone close, they're playing out their emotional trauma in public, usually for kicks. *Boring.*

RULE 5 ▶ DRUNKEN DECLARATIONS OF LOVE (AND HATE)

Keep your issues between yourselves! It's so boring for everyone when an argument is being shouted about on Facebook like a social-media version of *EastEnders.*

Here's Sophie and Geoff:

> **SOPHIE: Wow, Geoff is such a twat; he was reading through all the texts on my phone.**
>
> **GEOFF: Sophie is a knob. She told me to de-friend an ex.**

We get it. Geoff's a twat. Sophie's a knob. Now can we all get on with the important business of watching cats playing drums on YouTube, please?

RULE 6 ▶ BEWARE THE INAPPROPRIATE PHOTO

I recently posted a photo of my vlogging camera on Instagram with the caption, 'Me and you'. It was meant to represent the fact that I take my camera everywhere I go and share what I do with the viewers, while showing the equipment I use to make my videos. The filter was really arty too – I was pleased with the shot. What I hadn't realised when I'd placed the pic online was that the camera was nestling in my lap. *Awkward*. Every comment afterwards claimed I'd been taking crotch shots, which I hadn't, OK? *OK?!*

RULE 7 ▶ KEEP WORK AND LOVE SEPARATE ON SOCIAL MEDIA

Facebook for friends and relationships. Twitter for everything else. And don't be mates with your boss on Facebook because they'll see you at your worst. It's also worth remembering that whatever your legal rights to privacy, some companies have been known to go through the Facebook profiles of any potential employees after job interviews, so as much as you want to have a laugh online, always think, *If someone is going through my Facebook profile, what impression are they going to get?*

If you're photographed lifting trophies, helping old ladies across the road and doing volunteer work, then great. But those pics of you downing Jägerbombs might not be the best idea.

RULE 8 ▶ DON'T CHECK IN EVERYWHERE

My stepdad will check in literally every place he goes, even the petrol station, and it's a bit cringe, but it's so funny. He loves a good ol' check in, but you should keep a handle on it. Just think: you don't want to be seen as the person who brags about all those fancy places you've been to – like the McDonald's toilets.

RULE 9 ▶ PUT IT AWAY

You don't want to reveal *all* your private stuff to a load of strangers. I love sharing my life with my viewers on YouTube, but I do still have a privacy boundary that I feel is important. I think the intimate things, like parts of my relationship with Niomi, should be off limits. I don't film us kissing, for example. Some people do that with their partners and that's cool, but I want to keep things like that for us. Things that should be kept from the outside world include your partner's moles in strange places, the bed (and things that go on in it), weird lumps and bumps, and any toilet activities. Ugh.

Having said that, my audience is a great source of knowledge. Sometimes it's like having my own personal Wikipedia page. If ever I have something wrong, maybe an illness, I'll describe the symptoms in a video. Afterwards the comments section will be flooded with helpful suggestions and preventatives, all of them helping to restore my health to a hundred per cent.

RULE 10 ▶ SOCIAL MEDIA AND DRINK

The two don't mix. The amount of times I drunk-tweeted when I was younger was ridiculously frequent. The next day I'd almost always feel sick with embarrassment when I went through the tweets. Turn it off.

'A true relationship is someone who accepts your past, supports your present, loves you and encourages your future.'

– Thomas Edison

FIVE THINGS TO DO WHILE YOUR OTHER HALF GETS READY

1 ▶ WRITE A BOOK

In the time it usually takes Niomi to get her game face on, I could have written a few chapters for a *Twilight*-style literary sensation. Give it a go yourself. (I'm not comparing your loved one to the undead, by the way!)

2 ▶ DRAW A PICTURE

Get creative. Imagine what your other half is going to look like when they're finally done, then get it down on a pad with some crayons, or watercolours if you're feeling super-inspired. Hold your masterpiece up against them when they're finally finished and compare results. (Please feel free to tweet them to me.)

3 ▶ SING

Seriously, if you have a voice like mine, it'll speed the process along. You could even write a song about your partner getting ready. Because that won't be annoying at all.

4 ▶ WORK OUT

Maybe a few push-ups or burpees while your other half gets dressed? Just don't get too sweaty. You're going out, remember?

5 ▶ BOND WITH YOUR PETS

It's vital to create a happy environment for your animals, whether they're cats, goldfish or stick insects. This thirty-minute window (or an hour… or worse) is the perfect opportunity to get down with nature.

REBOOTING A BROKEN HEART

Hard life lesson #453: everyone will go through a break-up at some stage in their life and it's tough – really tough. It doesn't get any easier as you get older either. The most recent split can be as bad as the first, and people can hurt as much in their eighties and nineties as they do in their teens. The hardest thing is that it's easy to feel like the heartbreak is happening to you, and you only. If you lose a loved one in the family, there's usually a lot of other people grieving around you. When you've lost the love of your life, it's a pretty lonely business.

Some of my break-ups have been pretty bad, though luckily there haven't been too many to report. One girl, Sarah, kept cheating on me, and that was a nightmare. I kept hearing stories from other people about what she'd been doing, and my friends were urging me to drop her, but it was still really hard. Even though I felt wronged, I couldn't bring myself to do it.

Another girl I'd been with for six months dumped me out of the blue, and that was just as crap. I was young and though I wasn't in love, I still liked her. I had big feelings, and hearing that she wanted to end things was devastating. Of course she gave me the classic brush-off, telling me, 'It's not you, it's me.' So the next day, I decided to wallow in the misery for a while. I got maudlin, locking myself away while listening to a lot of depressing music. It was really horrible.

Dumping someone is a nasty experience as well; sometimes it's as bad as being dumped, if not worse. Why? Well, you probably still have feelings for the person you're breaking up with, and you might have no idea how they're going

'DUMPING SOMEONE IS A NASTY EXPERIENCE AS WELL; SOMETIMES IT'S AS BAD AS BEING DUMPED, IF NOT WORSE.'

to react. You feel guilty, too. When I was fourteen I decided to call it off with a girl I'd been with for a year, and I remember asking my sister to drop me off at her house because I was so scared to do it. I needed the emotional support. I don't think I've ever been so nervous than I was that day – I felt so weird.

When I finally got inside her front door, it took ages to get to the point. We chatted for a while until I eventually broke the news. Despite the fact I knew it was for the best, it was hard to put my feelings for her aside – to talk to her like a normal person without those emotions getting in the way. And I really didn't want to hit her with my decision straight away by saying, 'Yeah! Let's split up!' That would have been weird for her, and I would have felt awful.

When a break-up lands – as the dumper or the dumped – it can be an emotional roller coaster. You might feel sick; you'll want to cry. There will be a lot of sleepless nights, and plenty of stress for sure. Some days you might feel like sitting in your underwear all day, stuffing your face with pizza and chocolate (not at the same time please: you'll vom). Other days, getting out of bed might feel impossible.

It's important to remember that, in the end, you'll get back on track and feel like your old self again. But just in case you're struggling, I've put together a survival plan to get your heart on the mend, sooner rather than later...

1 ▶ RECOGNISE THE FIVE STAGES OF GRIEF

According to the experts, we all go through five phases in a break-up.

> #1 Denial: Yeah, they'll come crawling back...
>
> #2 Anger: WTF?! Why aren't they coming back?
>
> #3 Bargaining: Er, please come back!
>
> #4 Depression: Ugh, they're *so* not coming back,
> and no one will ever like me again...
>
> #5 Acceptance: Next!

Depending on the relationship and where your head's at, those stages might take days or weeks. They could even take months, years. Just ready yourself for a bumpy ride.

2 ▶ ALLOW YOURSELF TO FEEL CRAP...

Give yourself some time to wallow in the pain. Put some sad music on – Sam Smith maybe, or a bit of Ed Sheeran. Sit around watching weepy movies and eat a little comfort food. If you want to slob around all day and cry, do it. If you're going to hate on yourself, get it out of your system. When you do turn the corner – and you will – you'll have more confidence than ever before. Why? Well, you've gone through the worst and survived.

3 ▶ ...BUT SET YOURSELF A TIME LIMIT

Because sitting around in a onesie, watching crap TV and crying into your pizza six months down the line is not always a good thing.

4 ▶ PICK YOUR BREAK-UP SONGS CAREFULLY

Chances are you're going to listen to a lot of music during this very tricky time, so choose your playlists carefully, because whatever you're listening to, the emotions attached to the lyrics will stick. Don't be surprised if you find yourself in a nightclub years from now, feeling sad because the DJ's dropped that same song at the end of the night and it's brought back bad memories.

'MUSIC IS MEMORY, SO MAYBE DON'T LISTEN TO YOUR FAVOURITE BANDS DURING A LOVE SPLIT.'

I remember that my break-up anthem was 'Apologise' by One Republic. Just to crank up the heartache a little more, I streamed the acoustic version, which was slow and properly depressing. I was fifteen, and I remember walking along the street, the guitars ringing in my headphones, a tear or two in my eye. *Yeah, man,* I thought. *Tough times...*

The funny thing is, if I hear that song now, it takes me back to that very moment. Music is memory, so maybe don't listen to your favourite bands during a love split. You could ruin them for ever.

5 ▶ AVOID THE REBOUND

Some people love it, and they can do rebounds quite comfortably. They'll be going out the day after a break-up, on the pull again, like it's no big deal. But rebounding can be weird. Remember, you've been in a relationship with someone, so when you kiss another person it might whip up all sorts of feelings. It can bring more negative emotions on you. It might even make you miss the other person more. Don't dive in too quickly. Kiss carefully – that's all I'm saying.

6 ▶ DON'T LET YOUR GUARD DOWN

After a little while, you might feel great, back to your old self. You might think, *Yeah, I'm so over this*. Then, a couple of days later, you've returned to that bad place, and you're hiding from the world again. Understand that you might be in for some ups and downs – enjoy the ups, but look after yourself during the downs. Eventually it'll all level out and you'll be back to normal.

7 ▶ CUT YOUR SOCIAL MEDIA CONNECTIONS

If you're lucky enough not to work with your ex, or share classes, then cut all online contact as quickly as you can. Seriously, what's stopping you? Chop them from Facebook, Twitter, WhatsApp and Instagram, because you really don't want to see their latest photos, especially if they're having a great time without you (or worse, with someone else).

While you're at it, delete their emails, texts and contact numbers, too. You'll only be tempted to reread the smoochy ones, or message them in the middle of a crap day. And that rarely ends well.

8 ▶ REBUILD YOUR CONFIDENCE

You've taken a blow, you feel down, but the trick is to get your confidence pumping again. Go out and flirt. And I don't mean you should hit on someone in free period, or make a move on the first person you see in the staff canteen. I'm talking about a shared smile with someone on the street. Have a joke with the person next to you as you queue for a coffee (even if you don't fancy them). Get some chemistry going. It might not get you a date just yet, but it'll prove that there's life beyond your ex at least.

9 ▶ EXERCISE

Down in the dumps? Go for a walk with friends. Want to take your mind off feeling like a bit of a loner? Then play a game of football with mates. Feeling angry at being ditched? *Boom!* Take your anger out in a workout. Running is great, too. You'll be moving in the fresh air, lungs burning, and your endorphins will shoot up and you'll feel good about yourself. Even better, you'll look great, too. (Note: Not immediately afterwards. You'll be red-faced and sweaty.)

10 ▶ GET READY...

... because this is an exciting beginning. And it won't be long before you're experiencing all those amazing feelings of falling for someone again, but with a new person. Sure, it's easy to think, *Oh I'm gonna be on my own for ever now. I'm never going to meet someone else.* But put that thought process to one side and imagine a time when you can be happy again. The sooner you do that, the sooner someone will blow you away.

'A warm smile is the universal language of kindness.'

– William Arthur Ward

FRIENDS & FAMILY

CRISIS
SURVIVAL
GUIDE

Every day I learn a lot about the lives of my audience, and I'm often given a scary insight into just how tough things can be for young people. Whenever I make a video on a sensitive subject, I'm upset by the amount of people who respond by telling me that they're being bullied or that their parents are breaking up. Some of them have friends who have been self-harming and they're not sure how to help them. Others have mates who are changing emotionally and they're worried about losing friendships.

Listening and chatting to my viewers can be upsetting at times, but I always like to offer advice when I can, especially if that person is dealing with an issue on their own. Hopefully getting them to share their experiences with me and anyone else listening is a step towards fixing their problem. Whenever I record a new video that deals with a sensitive issue like bullying, I'm doing it in the hope that it will help people who are going through that very same thing.

I also want people to understand they're not alone. It's often easy for someone to think, *Oh, it's just me. This is my problem. Nobody else will understand. I'll get over it.* They keep their stress and hurt bottled up inside, but I know from experience that's the worst thing to do. It's far better to talk it out with someone. It can help so much. Even when I'm talking about my problems or dilemmas straight to the camera, I'm opening up to my audience. I'm releasing my emotions. It makes me feel better.

I'm not claiming to be an expert, or a counsellor here. I'm just a guy with a video camera and a YouTube channel. The thing is, I've been through some hard times myself in the past and I know just how helpful opening up can be, especially when life seems scary and unmanageable. My parents broke up when I was a kid and that was super-tough. I had to deal with the fallout of divorce with my two sisters, and I can still remember the tears and the stress, even though it's a little blurry now.

There have been deaths, too. All of my grandparents have passed away now, which is probably unusual for someone in their early twenties, and every loss was a huge hurt. I experienced bullying at school (albeit on a minor scale) and I nearly lost a close friend to anorexia, which was one of the most upsetting times of my life.

During those tough chapters, I've always had someone to turn to, whether that's my parents and my family, a teacher or a close friend. Every time, I've found that talking about my issues with another person has been a big help, especially if they were older and more experienced than me. It often set my mind at rest, or at least it helped me to deal with the stress of a situation as I learned how to navigate the sadness and fear I was feeling. Those people were a shoulder to lean on in some pretty grim moments.

This part of the book aims to do just that, but for you. Here, I've detailed the roughest incidents in my life so far – all of them full of hurt, worry, stress and fear. Some of the issues I've written about, like the loss of a loved one, are things that we all, sadly, have to face up to at some stage in our lives. Other stories are unique to me, but there might be incidents within them that you recognise in your own personal situation.

As well as my own recollections, I've also included some useful advice that I've learned along the way, in the hope that if ever you're faced with a similar challenge, I might be able to help you to deal with it better. Think of this section of the book as a crisis-management manual.

HOW TO SURVIVE A FAMILY BREAK-UP

I'll never forget the day Mum and Dad told me they were getting a divorce. I was about nine years old and it was awful. Dad picked me up from football training and my two sisters, Tash and Heidi, were in the car with him, but I had no idea anything was wrong at first. I was excited. The team had a big game the next day and I'd been picked to play, but I soon noticed a weird mood – I could feel it. Then Dad broke the silence.

> **'Mum and I need to talk to you all when we get home,' he said.**
> **I knew that meant trouble one way or another.**
> **'Er, Dad, what do you need to talk to us about?' I said.**

He told us it was important, but that he didn't want to say any more in the car, despite the fact we kept hassling him. We knew it was something heavy, though. Tash even asked outright if he and Mum were breaking up, but he still wouldn't say anything, so we all sat in silence feeling scared.

When we got home, Mum came in and sat us down on the sofa. That's when we were told the bad news.

One of our first family skiing holidays to Avoriaz in France

'We're getting a divorce,' she said.

Tash was probably around twelve then, old enough to understand what it all meant, and she freaked out and started crying. I didn't really get what was going on, and neither did Heidi, who was only about seven, but watching our older sister break down in tears made us cry, too. At first, Mum and Dad tried to convince us that everything was going to be cool, that nothing was going to change.

'Oh it's fine, it's not like anything bad's going to happen – we still love you,' said Dad.

But we all knew family life would never be the same again. How could it?

Looking back, I was young, I didn't see it coming, and the news hit me from out of nowhere. I guess that was a sign of good parenting, because the pair of them had managed to hide their issues and disagreements from us for so long. We certainly didn't see any fighting at home, not like you do with some break-ups. That didn't make the situation any less depressing, though, and Tash took it really badly. As soon as the awful reality had been explained to us, she ran to her room, with Heidi and me following her. We locked ourselves away for the evening as we tried to figure out what was going to happen to us.

'IT WAS HARD, AND ONCE THEY'D MOVED APART THERE WAS SO MUCH OF OUR LIVES TOGETHER THAT I BEGAN TO MISS.'

The one thing I remember is trying to stay positive, even on that nightmarish first day. I told the others that I thought Mum and Dad would work through it all – they had to, right? A while later, I kept saying to Heidi, 'Look, this could be cool. We're going to have two houses to mess around in. We're going to have Mum's house and Dad's house, and we'll spend three days at Dad's, four at Mum's. Dad even said we could get a trampoline at his house and a goal, so we can play football in the garden...'

Despite the optimism, life at home was tough for a while. There was a lot of heartache. I could see that Dad was really upset, and I'd tell him as often as I could that we all still loved him, but I don't think any of us understood what was going on. It was hard, and once they'd moved apart there was so much of our lives together that I began to miss. Like our bike rides into the country, or the holidays we used to go on as a family. I still saw Mum and Dad all the time, but the unity was gone because we never did anything together. Not the five of us anyway.

There was some glimmer of hope a year later. Though it's all a bit of a blur, the one vivid memory I have is of the three of us – Mum, Dad, me – in the park together. I was kicking a football against a fence, and they were chatting together. It looked pretty intense.

'What are you two talking about?' I asked, getting nosy.

Mum became evasive, but when I got into the car she blurted out the news. 'I think we're going to get back together again,' she said.

That made me so happy. But in the end it didn't work out for them, which was tough for all of us. Our hopes had been raised that life might get back to normal, and I hated seeing my parents sad again. I'd see them both upset and try to hug them. I'd say, 'Why are you upset?' But that made it even harder for them. Deep down they probably wanted to talk to me about it, but they couldn't. It wouldn't have been fair on any of us.

Life became even weirder once Mum and Dad started meeting different people – boyfriends, girlfriends. It was odd seeing them going out with new faces, and not all of them were nice. Mum started seeing one guy who me and my sisters hated, probably because he acted like he hated us. He'd swear at the three of us, and he was horrible to Mum, but what could I do? I was a little kid. I couldn't hit him or kick him out. I was just too young.

It got weird with Dad as well. He met someone new, they got married and she moved into our house with her sons. (I was living at Mum's but I was spending three days a week with Dad.) I admit it, I found that weird at first – really weird. I kept thinking to myself, *Stepbrothers? I don't know how I feel about this...* As they tried to settle into our way of life, I became very standoffish. The boys were called Matt and Tom, and it wasn't their fault that I was stressed out at the situation, or that I was reacting badly. I had a whole storm of emotions going on. I wasn't sure how to handle it at all.

Luckily I soon came around. I realised Matt and I shared the same interests. He was a year younger than me and we both loved basketball. We even liked the same teams. Dad had put up a hoop in the garden so we'd play together after school, trying different moves. In the end he became like a real brother to me. Even though Dad and his mum

Me and my stepbrother Matt, having a slice of pizza on a ski holiday

eventually broke up after a big wedding and six years of marriage, I still see him around Brighton and the banter is always the same. 'Oh, man,' I'll say. 'I miss you so much! Let's hang out.'

Despite everything that went on, we still have that relationship and a load of great memories together. Not everything that happened during the split was terrible.

'THE REALITY OF A BREAK-UP INVOLVING YOUR PARENTS IS THIS: IT SUCKS.'

Even though at the time I felt quite weird going through a family break-up, I now know that I wasn't in a minority. Loads of people I speak to these days have been through a divorce or a parental break-up. It might even be happening to you, which is why you're reading this chapter.

The reality of a break-up involving your parents is this: it sucks. But the biggest thing I learned from that time is how **DIVORCE CAN COME GOOD IN THE END**. That might sound crazy if it's happening to you right now, but it's true. My mum and dad both have new partners now, and they're both happy – maybe the happiest they've ever been in their lives. The fact that they're with different people was a little tricky to get my head around at first, but they've found people they're better suited to. And they still love my sisters and me as much as ever.

When the break-up was going on, I realised early on that it was important to **NEVER TAKE SIDES**. You might be at an age where your parents feel as if you're old enough to cope with the details, and as a kid that can be really daunting. Mum might moan about Dad; Dad might talk about something Mum's done to upset him. That can be heavy, so sit them both down and try this line: 'Mum, Dad, your problem is with each other. All I want is for you to be happy, so it would help if you don't bring me into it.'

It's a bold move and it might be hard to deliver, but it'll help in the long run.

Then remember that **THEY'RE HURTING, TOO**. The family has fallen apart so emotions are going to be flying around. There could be arguments, big fights. They might even say horrible things in front of you. But, deep down, they don't really mean any of it. Your parents have hit rock bottom. The good news is that the only way for them to go is up.

In the end I decided to **FIND SOMEONE ELSE TO CHAT TO**. I spoke to people I was close to who were older than me, like my year-four teacher. She knew what was going on because Dad had told her and one day she called me over at the end of a lesson. That gave me the fear at first because I didn't know what was going on. I thought I'd done something wrong.

Uh-oh, I thought, *I'm gonna be in trouble!*

But she then told me that she understood what was happening at home, and if I wanted to chat to her about it, I could. I found talking to her to be a massive help. Reaching out to someone with more experience than me was a boost. I felt supported. It was nice knowing she was there if ever I had to get something off my chest, especially if it was something I couldn't talk through with either Mum or Dad. I think dealing with it on my own might have been a bit of an ordeal.

'YOUR PARENTS HAVE HIT ROCK BOTTOM. THE GOOD NEWS IS THAT THE ONLY WAY FOR THEM TO GO IS UP.'

I guess the whole experience showed me that **MARRIAGE MIGHT NOT BE FOR EVERYONE**. I often feel like there's this pressure on all of us to eventually get married. There's still this idea that you have to live a traditional life, even though there are loads of people who are doing their own thing. Times are changing, which is really cool, so why rush into a marriage when it could end in divorce? Why even get married in the first place?

If you're into it, then great. If not, don't stress. And just because life might not have worked out in the way that your parents – and you – had hoped, it doesn't mean you can't all find happiness. I know, because that's what happened to me.

ILLNESS: HOW TO HANDLE THE STRAIN

One of the biggest challenges I've ever faced began a few years back when a family friend who I had known all my life and was close to at school (we'll call her Katy, although that's not her real name) became seriously ill. It started when she went to Thailand on holiday. She was only fourteen and travelling with a friend and her family, but one night, at the end of the trip, she sneaked out with her mate, like you do when you're a kid. The pair of them found a bar and ordered some drinks, but when Katy's mate went off with a random guy she was left alone. After that there were only flashbacks: some Australian guy, more drinks, her waking up in the middle of the street with memories of being in a stranger's apartment. It was nightmarish.

When Katy eventually found her way back to the hotel, she spent the night with her head in a toilet bowl, puking and passing in and out of consciousness. She was taken to hospital where a doctor told her that her drink had been spiked. They checked her for any signs of sexual assault, which thankfully hadn't happened, but she was freaked out at what turned out to be four missing hours. She had no idea of what had gone on, apart from blurry memories that would come out of nowhere, such as the recollection of a weird apartment and the feeling of some unknown man's hand on her back.

When I heard what had happened, I got really mad. I've always been very protective of Katy. I always used to stick up for her at school. The news made me livid and scared. I had loads of questions.

'Why her?'

'Are the police looking for this sicko?'

'How did this even happen?'

When Katy eventually returned home, she seemed fine at first. It was as if nothing that serious had really happened and we all brushed it off, hoping that was the end of it. It was only after four months or so that I noticed that she was acting a little strangely. It was just a few flashes at first, but she would leave her food at lunchtime, which was something she'd never done before. In the beginning it was just bits of her meal, then it was the whole plate. She would make out that she wasn't hungry.

Around the same time, Katy got into exercise – and I mean she *really* got into exercise. She would train all the time and at crazy hours of the day. One night her sister came downstairs around 2 a.m. to get a glass of water and found Katy skipping and dripping with sweat in the living room.

'Er, Katy, what are you doing?' she said.

'Oh I can't sleep,' said Katy. 'And Mum told me that skipping was a really good way to wear myself out.'

That made sense at the time. If you've got loads of energy and you can't relax, why wouldn't you exercise before going to sleep? But thinking about it now, we were forever being brushed off; Katy had an excuse for everything. If she wasn't eating, it was because she wasn't hungry. Exercising was her way of tiring her body so she could sleep more easily. Every weird incident had a legitimate explanation, until Katy admitted the awful truth to me: she had anorexia.

I guess it was a good thing that she had recognised the fact. She'd even booked herself a doctor's appointment to help resolve the issue. But it didn't feel like a positive start at the time. She told me that her condition had first started after coming back from Thailand. She would eat loads before making herself sick, which she knew was bulimia. Eventually she stopped eating altogether, and that's when the intense exercise regime began. Katy had wanted to be stick thin, but now she looked ill and tired. Anorexia was wasting her away.

It was to get even worse a short while afterwards when her parents went away for business one weekend and Katy asked me and some other friends to stay over. Hours after we'd all fallen asleep downstairs, I heard an awful scream coming from the bathroom. It was Katy. It was as if she was in real pain. I could tell by her voice that something was seriously wrong.

I ran in to see what had happened and when I pushed the door open the first thing I noticed was the blood. It was everywhere. Katy was standing there, a nasty-looking gash in her arm, and blood was pumping out of it. The cut was so deep I could almost see the muscle.

> **'What... what happened?' I asked, starting to get scared.**
> **'I was shaving my legs,' she said. 'I dropped the razor and then I fell on it. It sliced my arm open...'**

I should have known there and then that something was up, but I wasn't thinking straight. The blood and Katy's injury meant my focus was on driving her to the nearest A & E.

'Shall we call your mum?' I said, as we helped her into the car. Katy shook her head. 'No, I don't want to annoy her, Marcus. She's in Paris...'

'KATY WAS STANDING THERE, A NASTY-LOOKING GASH IN HER ARM, AND BLOOD WAS PUMPING OUT OF IT.'

It was only once we'd got Katy to hospital that the doubts started to creep in. A nurse was stitching up the cut and she soon started asking questions about how the accident had happened. Katy told her the exact same story as she had told me, but I could tell the nurse wasn't buying it.

'You're not lying to me, are you?' she said.

Katy was adamant. She explained for a second time that she'd fallen and cut herself on the dropped razor, but suddenly I was disbelieving her story, too. I think we all were. It didn't seem right. I called her mum later on in the early hours of the morning, and I remember saying, 'I'm not sure if it was an accident or not. I don't think a razor caused the cut, even though Katy swears it did...' The doubts were there in all of us.

After that, Katy's behaviour got progressively more dangerous. She collapsed at school one day and an ambulance was called out. I was later told by her mum that because she hadn't been eating, her energy levels were down to zero. Katy was wiped out. The doctors hadn't really solved the issue of her anorexia and none of us knew what to do. That's the moment when I first thought, *This is getting serious. This is bad.* But it was to get worse when I was at a house party with friends one evening and, as the night came to an end, I heard sobbing coming from the bathroom. It was Katy.

'Katy, what's up?' I said, knocking on the door. 'Is everything OK?'

When she let me in, Katy was sitting on the edge of the bath, crying. She told me that she had taken eight paracetamol, and she admitted to cutting her back. That made me nervous. I remembered our time in the hospital, the nurse's face, and Katy's story about the razor.

'THE DOCTORS HADN'T REALLY SOLVED THE ISSUE OF HER ANOREXIA AND NONE OF US KNEW WHAT TO DO.'

'What do you mean?' I said. 'Can I take a look?'

She turned round and lifted her T-shirt. I had to step back, hand across my mouth, just to hold it together. It looked bad. Her back was a criss-cross of slices and cuts. There was lots of blood and it looked like she'd been attacked by a cat – an angry one.

'Does it hurt?' I asked.

Katy nodded. 'Yeah, it really does...'

I asked her why she had done it to herself.

'Someone was telling me to do it,' said Katy. 'A voice in my head.'

She was crying a lot, unable to hold it together.

Now that *really* scared me. Katy was hearing things. It was getting late and I didn't want to leave her alone, so I took her back home and made sure she was going to be OK.

Not long afterwards, Katy was sectioned in a rehabilitation unit. She was only a teenager, but her condition was so serious that she was taken out of school for treatment. I remember visiting the clinic where she was staying and it was awful – there were ten other people in the ward and everyone was stick thin. I saw people sitting at tables, rocking backwards and forwards in their chairs. After they'd eaten their bodies would shake. I was only young. Those moments in the hospital opened me up to a whole new world.

Over the next six months there were different treatments for Katy. She went home for a while, then she was back in treatment for three months. When I visited her, I would often watch her as she ate her food because she would shake her legs while she was chewing. It was as if she had tonnes of nervous energy to use up, but I guess it was a symptom of the anorexia. She wanted to burn off the calories so she could stay thin, even though there was no weight on her at all. At times, I was worried we were going to lose her completely.

While Katy was away, I was told I could only speak to her once a week on the phone and she wouldn't be allowed out for visits. I would write letters to her instead, telling her

'SHE'S STUDYING FOR A DEGREE AND SHE'S HEALTHY AND SPORTY. SHE LOOKS AFTER HER BODY IN THE RIGHT WAY.'

how much I missed her and, over time, once friends were allowed to see her, I could see an improvement. She became happier. I caught her smiling. Katy was finding more energy and enthusiasm, turning back into the mate I remembered from before the illness took her away from us.

In the end, the doctors worked out that the root cause of her problems was the incident in Thailand. It had triggered post-traumatic stress disorder, which then brought on bulimia and anorexia, summoning up the devil in her head – the one she believed was telling her to be thin, to lose weight. There were no miracle cures they said, but with counselling and treatment Katy could manage her condition.

They were right, too. These days, she's great. She's studying for a degree and she's healthy and sporty. She looks after her body in the right way.

The thing is, we all know her condition isn't cured – it can't be. It's just being maintained – and we've all learned how to handle it, especially Katy. At times, though, life was really scary for me and my friends, and one of the main things I learned throughout the whole experience is that **IT'S IMPORTANT TO BE UNDERSTANDING**, though this can seem like the hardest thing in the world at the time. Often, when a loved one is going through something serious like a mental illness, it's not unusual to experience frustration, to think, *Why are they acting this way?*

That's natural. I studied mental illnesses in Psychology at college, which in no way makes me an expert, but it did give me an insight into what Katy was going through. I quickly realised that her condition was no different to someone with a broken arm or leg – they're injured, but in a different way. It was important for me to think, *How can I help her to live with this?* I realised she had a mental condition, and being understanding meant I could show an interest; I could care for her.

The other thing is **DON'T GET ANGRY**. It can be easier to show stress than concern. Why? Well, showing concern means you have to admit to yourself that something is terribly wrong, and that can be a scary thing to do. But, believe me, the ill person knows that

'BEING UNDERSTANDING MEANT I COULD SHOW AN INTEREST, I COULD CARE FOR HER.'

what they're doing is odd and scary to other people, yet they can't stop. They want to get better; they just don't know how to. Shouting at them, or asking 'What's wrong with you?!' every day isn't going to help. But love and understanding will.

It's also important to realise **THERE ARE NO QUICK FIXES**, or magic factory-reset buttons to restore a sense of balance and normality. Dealing with serious health issues can take time. So many people think that if you go to the doctor to gets some pills, it'll all be OK. But working with a mental illness is one of the most complex things out there. It takes time.

IT'S IMPORTANT TO LOOK OUT FOR YOUR FRIENDS OR LOVED ONES. Often they'll want your help when they're in trouble. I know Katy did. It could be that you've noticed a mate at school rapidly losing weight, or that strange cuts are appearing on their body. People will often gossip to their friends about someone acting a little odd, but they rarely ask if they can help that person. If it's your friend, don't let them slip away. Don't get in their face about it, but do reach out and find out what's going on.

Of course, they might not want to talk to you at first. They might even shout at you. You've got to almost accept that an argument or confrontation could happen because they're feeling scared or embarrassed. They might be in denial about the situation, but deep down they'll want help. If a one-on-one conversation doesn't work and you know something's seriously wrong, then explain the situation to a parent or teacher. They'll know the best thing to do.

If you are worried about someone who is very close to you and part of your immediate family or friendship group, remember: **EVERYONE AROUND YOU WILL BE WORRIED.** If a sibling or relative is really sick, your dad could become stressed and your mum might freak out. If it's someone close to you at school, a lot of your friends might become upset. Consider that when tempers become frayed, or people appear to be down or edgy. It's natural for everyone to feel unbalanced.

'WORKING WITH A MENTAL ILLNESS IS ONE OF THE MOST COMPLEX THINGS OUT THERE. IT TAKES TIME.'

There will come a time when the problem is resolved, though. A lot of people recover from serious illnesses or mental-health issues, but sometimes that isn't the end of the process. Like with Katy. She isn't cured; she's simply learned how to **MANAGE THE SITUATION**, and it's important that you learn how to manage it, too.

Once a person starts getting better, that's when the hard work starts: they're going to need support from their friends and family, more than you can imagine. I remember when Katy came back from rehab, her family were there to help her, as were her mates. We were supportive. We respected her and made sure she knew that we understood her situation. That gave her the confidence to go forwards.

It's very easy for someone returning from a serious illness to feel paranoid. Katy could quite easily have felt scared about returning home. She might have thought, *Oh god, I've got to go back. My friends and family don't get it. They hate me. They might shout at me...* But as her friends we understood that something was wrong. We had to do everything we could to support someone we loved very much.

If you're in the same situation as I was, remember to make the person in trouble feel loved and welcome. Tell them you understand. Tell them you love them. The best thing you can do for that person is to let them know that you'll be there for them, no matter what happens.

DITCHING TOXIC FRIENDS

Sometimes, if you choose them badly, your friends can cause you as much stress as your enemies. Trust me, I know from experience. For a short while when I was at school, I used to hang around with the naughty kids. They were the troublemakers in the year for sure, and though I wasn't usually a badly behaved kid myself, for a while I found myself getting a buzz out of getting into scrapes with them. I started skiving and messing around in class and picking up detentions and warnings from teachers.

It wasn't really bad stuff – I wasn't into fighting, stealing or bullying – but I was putting pins on teachers' chairs so they would jump up when they sat on them. I'd get wet toilet tissue, run past the school kitchen, ring the door bell so someone would come and open the door, and then launch the wet tissue towards the staff. I even threw rocks at windows until they cracked – those kinds of things. Looking back, it wasn't that much of a big deal. It was hardly crime-of-the-century stuff, but I guess it could have been a gateway to some more serious issues, had I not got it under control and stepped away from that group. That was a decision I had to make, and leaving them behind was tough. They were fun; they made me laugh. I can remember some good times hanging out with those guys, but deep down I knew what I was doing wasn't right. I also realised I could get into a lot more trouble at school if I didn't sort my attitude out. There wasn't one incident that forced me into that decision – it was a gradual realisation.

It wasn't an easy thing to do, and to figure out whether I should stick with them I had to ask some serious questions of myself, like: a) What are these people doing for me? b) What are they bringing to my life? and c) Am I hanging around with them because they're the cool kids at school, or because I value and trust their friendship?

My answers were as follows:

a) They're getting me into trouble at school (for being a bit of a dick).
b) I'm getting grief for being in trouble at school (for being a bit of a dick).
c) Because they're the cool kids in school, rather than close personal friends (and I'm becoming a bit of a dick).

That's when I made the decision to stop hanging out with them. It was a bit awkward but I realised it was for the best in the long run. In the end I stopped messing around with them, I quit skipping classes, and a lot less trouble came my way as a result. I also decided that it was better to have a smaller number of friends who were 'real', rather than a big group of cool people who might say things behind my back, or weren't entirely trustworthy.

The toughest hurdle to overcome was fear. I worried I might not have any friends at all after I'd made the break. It's easy to think that way and everyone does it, but I needed to overcome my anxiety about the future. I needed to believe that I could walk away and find new mates, or focus on the good friends I already had.

If you're in the same situation as I was, you can do the same, too. You have to make a change and walk away from the people who are bringing you down and negatively affecting your life. It will be weird at first. They might take it badly. You might have to spend free time at college or work on your own for a while, but that loneliness won't last. You'll improve your relationships with long-lasting friends. You'll probably meet new people because the chances are you'll put yourself out there to meet different faces (but remember your mistakes from last time).

'YOU HAVE TO MAKE A CHANGE AND WALK AWAY FROM THE PEOPLE WHO ARE BRINGING YOU DOWN.'

Even if you can't – if you're shy, say – new friends will come around eventually. It won't be long before you're thinking, *Wow, remember that knobhead who got me into all that trouble at uni? Where are they now?*

BEWARE THE PACK MENTALITY

It's easy to become a bullying presence, without really knowing it. Often in a gang of people there's one domineering voice – the one person who shouts louder than all the others. Usually they're the person everyone follows, often because they're the boldest rather than the wisest; they're decision makers by default.

That's fine if they're a positive force, but if they're not so nice, they can often cause a situation, because at times domineering people can become bullies. That's particularly unpleasant if they have an issue with you. They can turn the group against you; pushing your buttons becomes fun for them. Before you know it, they've brought you down in front of your mates and peers and you're feeling crap about yourself.

It's even worse, however, when they encourage *you* to behave horribly – to pick on someone else, sometimes without even realising it. When a group of friends you're in is bullying someone, it can be easy to get dragged into that pack mentality. After all, rather someone else than you, yeah? But think about it this way: is that how you really want to go through life? How would you feel if you were the kid being emotionally hassled all the time? I know I'd hate it.

I don't want to sound like your parents here, but my advice would be to step out of the situation. If you know you're being influenced into bad things, stop and think, *Is this right? Would I be doing this if it wasn't for the group? Am I doing this to prove a point and be cool?*

Often the simple answer is to stand up to the domineering voice, the bully, and bring them down a notch. But sometimes that's tricky (especially if they're huge). Meanwhile, if the other people in the group don't want to quit their unpleasant behaviour, you might have to step away on your own. It's a big deal, but think of the bigger picture. Your bold move might prove awkward and scary at first, but you'll be glad you did it in the long run.

THE FIVE FRIENDS IT'S COOL TO HAVE

OK, so you've spring-cleaned your social life. You've brushed away the cynicism, trouble and stress of your toxic 'mates'. What now? How about looking out for a couple of the five types of people who are great to lean on in hard times...

1 ▶ THE ADVICE SPECIALIST

The go-to person if you're experiencing a major personal problem – a dispute with your other half, for example, or an issue at home that you can't chat to your parents about. The Advice Specialist is wise beyond their years – like a cooler older brother or sister. Somehow they know exactly the best thing to do or say in any given situation.

It's not just the heavy stuff they're skilled in dealing with; it can be the trite and trivial, too. Need to deal with a troublesome flatmate? They'll know how to negotiate the issue. Need a new pair of football boots? They'll have a tip for the best deal on the market. Brown or black as the colour this season? They'll have it nailed already, plus they also know the best places to shop. These people are the Yoda of the college common room, the Zen master of the staff canteen. You should make the most of their wisdom.

2 ▶ THE INFO SPONGE

Your most knowledgeable friend, and the kind of person who should appear on a quiz show – a pub quiz champ-in-waiting. The Info Sponge is a font of all knowledge – useful and not so useful.

In fact, random truths are their speciality. They're the sort of person with whom you have those deep conversations about how Planet Earth formed and how we all got here today. You start to drift off and talk about aliens, galaxies and how old the earth is. You ask: 'How long have humans ruled the earth?', 'Why is the sky blue?' and 'What even is rain?' There's a bit of umming and ahhing and a lot of weird suggestions and ideas. Then the Sponge out of nowhere comes up with the answer and backs it up with their scientific technical reasons. My mate Jim

Climbing trees in Norwich with Jim

Chapman is the Info Sponge. I can ask him anything and he'll know the answer. Even if he's unsure he'll usually be able to blag his way through. He's more Google than human.

3 ▶ THE RISK-TAKER

There are two sides to the Risk-taker: always good for fun, but only in small doses, the Risk-taker is great to hang around if you're a thrill-seeker, but not so good if you're of a nervous disposition or easily led into trouble. Some of the things the Risk-taker gets up to are often a bit much for the 'normal' person.

In later life, the Risk-taker is the kind of person who'll jump into business decisions. They'll take the financial chance that other people are too scared to consider – and they might win, they might lose. As a young person, he or she will love bungee-jumping and tequila slammers.

I have a friend called FunForLouis – aka Louis Cole – who falls into the Risk-taker category. He travels the world doing the most insane things. Most of the time he films his madness and then puts it online for the rest of the world to see, and his stuff is full on. One day he's in Dubai jumping out of a plane, the next day he's flying to Brazil and hiking in the jungle for three weeks. He lives an amazing life, living life to the full and exploring the world.

4 ▶ THE JOKER

The person who makes you laugh the hardest. They're funny in any situation, sometimes inappropriately. At other times they'll crack you up with a funny story, or a witty response. At times, the Joker might be unintentionally funny, but they're always on hand in times of stress.

I have two groups of mates, my best mates from school and my YouTube mates. Out of my YouTube friends, the Joker is probably Joe Sugg. He has his own sense of humour, and he won't mind me telling you that it's the weirdest thing. Joe is in his own little world most of the time and when you're in conversation with him you never really know if he's being serious of not. He's known for really crap jokes but they're so crap they're funny. My attitude to Joe's 'humour'? If in doubt, laugh.

Joe and me, with soaking wet, sad faces

My mate Dave also falls into this category, purely based on the fact that most of the time he has no idea he's being funny. It's the things he does and his lack of common sense in group situations that almost make you laugh at him, in a fun way of course.

5 ▶ THE BLUNT INSTRUMENT

This is the friend who speaks their mind about everything. They rarely think, *Hmm, should I say that?* As a result, the Blunt Instrument won't hold back; they'll just tell it how it is. Of course, that won't always make them the most popular person in the group. And there's a good chance they'll offend people occasionally, but most of the time they're just saying what everyone else is thinking. The only difference is that the Blunt Instrument has the courage to say it.

One of the first pictures from when I went travelling with Max

I don't mean that in a bullying way. The Blunt Instrument is the type of person who will openly question why you're wearing cowboy boots* as a serious fashion choice, rather than talking about it behind your back with other people. If ever you're getting carried away, or too cocky, the Blunt Instrument can bring you back down to earth. They'll call you out. And though what they've said might hurt initially, you can rest assured that they've done you a favour in the long run. This is my mate Max through and through. Ever since I've known him he's been great at making things slightly awkward in a group confrontation. He doesn't really hold back. Most of the time he's saying what's on everyone's minds though.

* I've never worn cowboy boots.

THE INTERNET FOR OLD(ER) PEOPLE

We all know the internet is an amazing world, but it can also be a strange and nightmarish place. And it's almost guaranteed to blow the minds of people from a different generation. By that I mean anyone over the age of seventy – you know, old people like your gran. Though of course I'm not being ageist here; older people can use the internet, too.

'I USED TO GET HUNDREDS OF THOUSANDS OF HITS WITH EVERY NEW VIDEO.'

What I'm saying is that the internet can be a bit of a head-melt if you're not used to it. I know my mum and dad were a bit confused when I started making YouTube videos, and rightly so. There were times when people were coming out of nowhere, offering cash for advertising slots on an early working channel of mine. My parents were concerned about where it all might be heading. The papers were full of horror stories about kids getting sucked into trouble on the internet, and it was probably a bit worrying for them.

I guess I was a bit weirded out by the attention, too. I was sixteen and being a bit naughty, uploading music clips from other websites only available in the UK. I used to rip clips from official sites and put them up on my YouTube channel, basically so people outside Britain could see the clips, too. I used to get hundreds of thousands of hits with every new video. My head was spinning, though I don't think my parents really knew what to make of it all.

I can't blame them really. I was up to all kinds of madness online. As Marcus Butler TV began to take off, I started pulling crazy stunts in front of my camera, or performing wacky pranks whenever I hit a landmark

Sixteen-year-old me trying to find my destiny - haha!

subscription number – like 1,000 subscribers or 2,000. These are small figures compared to what I have now, but back in the day they felt like a huge deal.

I'll never forget the time I landed my 5,000th subscriber. I was hyped, super-excited. The event happened on my final day at college and it had taken me two years to get to that number. With my exam books handed in, and a holiday with my parents starting the following day, I wanted to celebrate in style, so I decided to dye my hair pink on video.

God knows what my mum must have thought as she saw my mate Tom in the garden, rubber gloves on, rubbing pink hair dye into my skull in front of a video camera. She probably became even more confused hearing me wailing from the bathroom an hour or so later. After five washes, my blond locks were still a fluorescent shade.

'Er, Mum, why is my hair still pink?' I shouted.

Mum scanned the instructions on the packet. The news wasn't good.

'Marcus! It says here "Semi-permanent"!' she said, not sounding too pleased. 'It can last, on average, six to eight weeks.'

I'd blown it – big time. I spent the next two weeks looking like an absolute weirdo on holiday, walking around with a dodgy shade of pink hair as everyone stared at me and sniggered. Niomi was not pleased.

When I thought it was a good idea to dye my hair bright pink and fake tan for 5,000 subscribers...

Me looking very unimpressed with my pink hair on holiday

I was unfazed by my fail, and the stunts over the next few months and years became more outlandish, more adventurous (they're still online if you want to see them). But as my channel got bigger I was forever hearing the same stuff about my time online from family and friends:

'What are you doing?'
'You're just filming yourself and putting it online and people are watching this?'
'Hang on, this is a weird video thing that you do and you put it on the internet?'
'Who the hell is watching this?'

I guess some of their concerns were fair. To the older, outside world what I was doing might have looked a little nuts. Some of their worries – like whether I had scary, pervy viewers – while being natural questions for people who didn't really understand social media, or websites like YouTube, were explained away with conversation and a little common sense.

Your parents might have the same concerns. They might be worried that you've hooked up to my channel, or that you're friends with so many people on Facebook, so over the next few pages I'm going to show you how to remove their fears. Please feel free to use the following parent-friendly explanations as a cut-out-and-keep crib sheet for dealing with any webophobic (© Marcus Butler) family members at your next Christmas party.

1 ▶ 'THE INTERNET IS SUCH A SCARY PLACE…'

I'd imagine that as a parent letting your kid loose online can be worrying. The stuff you can access with your fingertips is pretty terrifying – not that I've looked. But once you've got it into your parents' heads that the internet is a fascinating and useful tool, not only for work but for education and social media, too, they should come around. I always found it was helpful to show them what I was looking at online. Well, most of the time.

2 ▶ 'WE JUST BURIED THE CAT – LOL MUM xxx'

Warning #1: Your parents will try to use internet slang, they will get it wrong, and it will be a bit cringe. So ease their pain by outlining the basic

chat techniques. That way, they won't embarrass you, or themselves, in public. So, for example: 'Mum, LOL means "laugh out loud" rather than "lots of love". But thanks for telling me about the cat.'

Warning #2: You'll inevitably become bombarded with their new all-over-the-place lingo in a series of weird texts, with added inappropriate emojis – bananas, the dreaded turd symbol, etc. Just don't teach them too much. You'll want to keep back a secret code for yourself, just in case of emergencies.

3 ▶ 'HANG ON, YOU MET YOUR NEW GIRLFRIEND/BOYFRIEND... ONLINE?'

Any dating site is difficult to explain to someone who is unfamiliar with it, because they tend to think, *How can you meet someone and build a relationship through social media?* It's a societal change some parents just can't get their heads around, like Spotify or Twitter. For other parents, those that are single, say, internet dating might be all too familiar to them. Just try not to think about that too much if your mum or dad are single and looking for love. It might gross you out a bit.

The way to explain it to them is this: 'Mum, Dad, with online dating you can establish what you like and don't like in a relationship so nobody's time is wasted. You can also find out important things about the person you're about to date, things it might take two or three dates to establish in person. And, yes, the person I'm meeting might be weird, but then a person I've met at a party might be weird, too. At least online I can talk to them at length to find out whether they're nuts or not, check out their friends on Facebook, and build up an idea of what they're like.'

Just watch yourself for stalking tendencies when you're doing your research, though. No one likes a stalker. Look at your date's photos if they're online. But don't go too far.

4 ▶ 'SHOULD YOU REALLY BE DOING YOUR HOMEWORK ON THE INTERNET?'

Oh my god, yes! I once asked Mum how she used to do her homework back in the day. The conversation went a little like this...

> ME: Mum, when you were studying plate tectonics in the San Andreas Fault for Geography, where did you get the information?
> MUM: The library. To get there, I used to walk six miles in my plimsoles, which had holes in.
> ME: Misshhhh. And what if that book wasn't there?
> MUM: I'd have to wait a week for it to come back in...

So there you have it: seven days of research versus ten seconds on Google. A no-brainer in other words. Just don't tell them you're copying and pasting *all* your essay answers in one hit, though. I'm sure that might cause a few issues.

5 ▶ 'CAN WE BE FACEBOOK FRIENDS?'

The question nobody wants to hear from a parent. Of course they want to check up on you and make sure you're safe. Of course they want to find out if you've got drunk or skived school. And of course you would be within your rights to say 'No', and point them towards Twitter instead.

> 'Mum, Dad,' I told my parents when they asked me, 'why don't you follow me on Twitter? I'm always tweeting, and you'll know where I am and what I'm doing. It'll tell you that I'm all right.'

Much better they see my posts of no more than 140 characters than Facebook, where a naked holiday photograph, taken while drunk in Ibiza and covered in suncream, might surface at the worst possible moment.*

* Note to Mum and Niomi: there is no naked holiday photograph taken while drunk in Ibiza and covered in suncream. Honest.

Halloween in Sydney. Yes, that is me in a bin bag.

⊠ IMPORTANT!

It goes without saying that you should be clued up on internet safety. Never give your bank details to strange people claiming they want you to inherit their millions. Also, be aware that people you meet online are not always who they say they are, and in extreme cases, social media relationships can be very dangerous. If you're under the age of sixteen, never meet up with a stranger. Even when you're a bit older, still be careful – if it's a date, meet in a very public place and let someone know your plans. Always be cautious when accepting emails, or opening attachments – they may carry viruses. And if anyone ever asks you to do something that makes you feel uncomfortable or worried, tell a parent or teacher.

CONQUERING TROLLS AND BULLIES

One of the biggest regrets I have is that on the one occasion I was bullied, I gave in to the people who were tormenting me.

I was still at school, a teenager, and all my life I'd been pretty sporty. I was in the school football team and I ended up playing for Seagulls, the academy side for the professional team, Brighton & Hove Albion. I was good at basketball, too; I played for the county and seriously considered trying to get a college scholarship in America. Judo, rugby, tennis: you name it, I'd try to get involved with it.

Gymnastics was my biggest talent, though. I got into it when I was young and by the time I was fourteen I'd been crowned Sussex champion three times. Floor and vault were my specialities and nobody came close to me at school. At county level I was ahead of most people, too. I loved team sports as a kid, but I really loved winning, and at gymnastics I was a serious performer.

Maybe that was my biggest problem: I was a champ in a solo sport, and one that I guess could be considered a little unusual. Kids at school started taking the mickey out of me for giving up my time to compete in a sport that wasn't considered cool, like football. I would get rinsed every day for being a gymnast, and for wearing Lycra (which every gymnast has to wear, and most athletes, too). They called me 'gay' on the school field (there's nothing wrong with that), and a 'girl' (there's nothing wrong with that either, by the way), and though neither of those things bothered me individually, the combined stress got to me.

Competing for Brighton and Hove gymnastics at the Sussex county championships. I came first :D

'I HATED KNOWING THAT NO MATTER WHAT I DID, A CERTAIN GROUP OF KIDS WERE GOING TO GIVE ME CRAP FOR BEING GOOD AT A SPORT I LOVED DOING.'

The name-calling was happening every day and it brought with it a pressure I'd never experienced before. I hated knowing that no matter what I did, a certain group of kids were going to give me crap for being good at a sport I loved doing. Sure, it was a little bit unusual, but I never understood how people could be so disrespectful, hurtful and horrible to another person, another human, just for fun. It really sucked.

I know it could have been a lot worse – especially today. I went to school at a time when online bullying didn't really exist. Looking at the abuse I hear some of my viewers have gone through, I'm shocked at the level of meanness.

It's as if people change their persona online. They become someone different. They can act so cruelly, probably because there's no barrier. They can say whatever they want through a keyboard or a phone and there's no emotional comeback. They don't see the pain in the other person's face; they won't see them crying over their laptop. Often they won't get told off for doing it, because people in schools, colleges and workplaces haven't taken it that seriously. Not until now anyway.

Though their methods of bullying were different, the kids who were making my life hell had the same intentions as any online bully. They couldn't understand what I was doing and why I liked it. They were also probably a bit jealous of the fact I was winning county championships. I could do backflips at parties, where people would tell me what I was doing was 'really cool'. But this one group reacted like certain people do when they experience jealousy: they turned on me.

It wasn't so bad at first; their insults just bounced off me. But after a while of having horrible words thrown at me, I gave them what they wanted: a victory. I quit gymnastics. I told Mum, Dad and my coach I didn't want to carry on and I turned my back on the sport I loved.

It's easy to say it now, but I should have gone to my parents for help. They would have known how best to handle the situation, but I was worried about how they were going to react. I didn't want them to call the school or, worse, the other kids' parents. And I really didn't want to be called into a meeting where all the bullies would be told by the teachers that they had to leave me alone. After that, people would have thought of me as being a snitch, which wouldn't have helped at all. In my mind, the issue was only going to get worse unless I caved in.

Giving up was the worst thing I could have done. What I've learned since is that bending to their will is exactly what the bully wants. It fuels their ego. Whereas had I stuck to my guns, I would have infuriated them initially and then, when it was clear they couldn't influence me, they'd have got bored and moved on. Had I ignored them or gone for help, they would have left me alone eventually.

'HAD I IGNORED THEM OR GONE FOR HELP, THEY WOULD HAVE LEFT ME ALONE EVENTUALLY.'

Mum and Dad would have told me that, had I found the courage to explain my problem to them. Mum would have said, 'Marcus, they're jealous of you. You can do all this stuff that they can't. You're winning competitions, you're having fun, you're a champion. Don't let it get to you.' Instead I became scared of opening up. I bottled it when it came to asking for help. Potentially I could have gone far with gymnastics. But at the crunch moment I gave into bullies and I massively regret that decision now.

You can be stronger than me. You don't have to cave in to the people who are rinsing you for doing something you truly love, and I feel really passionate about that. When someone has a unique talent, they shouldn't have to worry about other kids, or adults, bringing them down. Especially if it's something quirky, like origami, chess or even gymnastics. Learn from my mistakes. Don't let the pressure get in your way. Try to keep an end goal in sight.

I know what you're thinking: *Easier said that done.* Well, let me give you a step-by-step guide to how to deal with a bully.

1 ▶ KNOW YOUR ENEMY

Your bully is weak. Your bully is afraid and insecure. Sure, they might be clever or physically strong, but deep down some unknown fear is eating away at them. Something frightens them. Why else do bullies hunt in packs? Because they need other people and opinions – usually from people even weaker than they are – to give them back-up or reinforcement.

In real life – the playground, common room or workplace – people side with bullies because they're afraid of being a target themselves. Online it's different; it's where the troll comes into play. Trolls are people who deliberately post negative comments on message boards and internet groups. They might be anonymous strangers, or they could be people you know, and they tend to influence people's actions with a keyboard. They use their opinions to bring someone they don't like down. That might be someone who's posting their own music videos online, or a wannabe video-maker putting up their latest project. The troll sees them making strides, being brave, and decides to cut them down for fun.

Now, before I go on, I think it's good to share opinions. Everyone has them, and everyone should feel confident in expressing them, providing those views are positive. But if those opinions are poisonous, they can quickly affect thought on a large scale and bring someone down. That can cause a lot of pain.

Social media and the internet are easy places to foster a pack mentality. In real life, bullying on a large scale is harder to organise because most people don't like it. It angers or upsets them. They see another person getting attacked by a group and they don't like it. They see a reaction in the target and they feel bad.

That's not the case online. The pain isn't visible to an audience because the person being trolled is hidden away, in their bedroom, unable to fight back. Because there's no comeback, the troll often feels invincible. No one's going to come back on them and front them up.

That's the theory anyway, but it won't make your enemy vanish overnight sadly, so here comes the practical stuff...

'IN REAL LIFE – THE PLAYGROUND, COMMON ROOM OR WORKPLACE – PEOPLE SIDE WITH BULLIES BECAUSE THEY'RE AFRAID OF BEING A TARGET THEMSELVES.'

2 ▶ IGNORE THEM

Your bully or troll is after a reaction. They want you to get upset and they want you to freak out. In my case, they wanted to manipulate me into giving up something I was good at – and I allowed them to win. I've learned from my mistakes though and the best way to beat them is to ignore them. Yeah, I know that's what every friend, parent and teacher will tell you to do, and it seems almost impossible at first, but, trust me, it works.

If you're thinking, *Fine, Marcus, but what do you know? You gave up when you were bullied...* Believe me when I tell you I get abuse every day online. Whenever I post a new video on YouTube, there are always negative comments. For a while there was one person who started regularly hating on me across everything, usually less than a day after I'd uploaded something new.

It got to me at first. I started to recognise their name whenever it appeared in the comments section of a video. In the end I started waiting for their comments because I knew they were inevitable. But the thing with me is, I learned my lesson from school. I knew not to give in. Eventually I figured, *You know what? Are they achieving anything from doing this? Nope. And if they don't like me, why do they watch every video I post?* I just reached for the online equivalent of ignoring them. I clicked the block button and didn't hear from that troll again.

3 ▶ GET HELP

If the above hasn't sorted the situation, it's time to reach out for the big guns: a helping hand, which I know feels like the last thing you want to be doing right now. Why? Well, I guess it can make you feel as if you can't handle the situation on your own, or that you're not as strong as you thought you were. You'll also be aware that there might be consequences to your actions. People might think of you as a rat. The bully or trolls might come back at you harder than before.

This fear is what they're banking on. They're expecting you to be too frightened to ask for advice, or to get someone to stop their actions. They think you'll be worried that your parents won't understand, especially if it's an online issue, that you'll suspect that your parents won't take it seriously given it's something they haven't gone through themselves. Whether it's online or not, if you're experiencing trouble, you should explain to a parent, teacher or colleague that you're being put through hell and you need some help. Doing this is the first step towards happiness because talking about it will: a) help you to release some pent-up emotion, and b) that person will help you to make the first steps to improving your life, whatever they might be.

Be brave, and good luck. If you're at step two without an answer, turning for help is the best solution, and one you'll be thankful for in the long run. I know from experience. I wish I'd reached out when I was giving up on my dreams. Don't let the bullies win like I did.

What I've given you is just the anti-bullying basics. If you want some more detailed advice or info on your problem, visit the following websites:

The Anti-Bullying
Ambassadors
antibullyingpro.com

Anti-Bullying Alliance
anti-bullyingalliance.
org.uk

Government
stopbullying.gov/kids/

DEALING WITH LOSS

I don't have any grandparents any more. I guess for someone my age that's probably quite unusual, and while I was growing up there weren't any significant older men in the family – apart from Dad and Simon (my stepdad), who are great, of course – which was a massive shame. Dad's father had passed away before I was born. Mum's dad died when she was seventeen, which was huge for her. She told me that they had been really close. So growing up I only had grandmothers in my life, but they were very important to me.

I have to admit, though, looking back, I feel I missed out on certain grandfather opportunities. I'd hear friends talking about their granddads at school and what they'd been up to, like fishing, learning to play snooker or whatever, and

I'd think, *I wish I had a granddad. I wish I could experience what it's like having that grandson–grandfather relationship.* But I was never bitter about it. I just took it as a life experience that I wasn't going to get, and I enjoyed the stuff that was there for me instead.

Like Granny. She was Mum's mother, and I loved her very much, but when I was about eight she was diagnosed with Alzheimer's disease, which was

Granny to the left; Grandma on the right

a condition that affected her memory, among other things. There were no significant symptoms at first, and my sisters and I would even talk to her about it, but as we got older her condition deteriorated.

Granny's mental state started to get worse – much worse – when I was about thirteen. At the time she was living in her old house, and there was one occasion when Mum visited her and she wasn't there. Mum rang around to find out if anyone had seen her, or if she was visiting one of her friends, but after an hour or so of asking questions it was obvious nobody knew where she was. Everyone was concerned.

We called the police, who eventually found her, and it turned out that she had gone on one of her walks, which she loved to do. This time, though, she had walked about four miles away from her home and couldn't work out where the hell she was. Granny's mind had become confused and she wasn't able to find her way home. It must have been so terrifying for her.

It freaked me out as well. I remember thinking, *Whoa, this is Granny. I've grown up with her being strong and independent, but now I can see she's not functioning right. This is horrible...*

It got worse. I could see that her brain was being destroyed by the disease, that her memories were going with it. She started forgetting my name, my sisters' names; sometimes she wouldn't recognise us at all. In the end she had to go into a specialist care home and everyone would take turns looking after her. Granny was going into a downward spiral, and it was awful for all of us, but it was so tough on Mum, working full time, raising kids and having to look after her mum, too.

I think the fact that it was a slow process made it a little easier to handle – not that it was easy by any stretch of the imagination. I think in the back of my head I always knew that she might get worse, and that she could pass away from her condition. I suppose that time meant I was able to prepare myself for the awful reality of it all, but it didn't make her dying any less devastating. I was sixteen, it was heartbreaking, and I took the news very hard.

'SHE STARTED FORGETTING MY NAME, MY SISTERS' NAMES; SOMETIMES SHE WOULDN'T RECOGNISE US AT ALL.'

With my grandma, it was different. Her death happened quickly, and it was just as horrible. She was a grandparent I'd had an amazing relationship with. My sisters and I would spend all summer with her; Mum would drop us off in the morning while she went to work, and as soon as we got to Grandma's house we'd convince her to take us to the sweet shop.

'Mum said we could go,' we'd say.

Grandma would always question us. 'Are you sure?' she would say, though she knew she was going to take us anyway. 'Oh, all right then...' And off we'd go, walking along Brighton Pier where she would give us money to play on the machines or jump around on the trampolines. We spent so much time with her as kids. She'd even come on holiday with us, or go on walking trips with the family.

But there was always some doubt in her about her own mortality that I found strange. She would sometimes say, out of the blue, 'Oh I'll die soon.' Even at sixteen I would put her straight, telling her, 'What are you talking about, Grandma? You're an eighty-year-old woman and you're still walking up hills! You're healthy! You'll live a long life!' So it was a massive shock to hear one day that she had had a fall in her house, a really bad one, and that she'd had to go to hospital.

After that, I remember thinking that she was starting looking old, like a little old lady. She had always looked strong and healthy before. I wondered if the fall had affected her, or knocked her confidence. She wasn't herself any more and it wasn't long before the falls became a more common occurrence. There was another incident on a bus that scared us all. Then we learned that she was having heart problems and needed to take all these pills. One night, all of a sudden, she got really sick and was put into hospital.

Tash and I were worried (Heidi was in America at the time). Tash called me to tell me the news, but neither of us really knew how serious it was. We went over to the hospital as soon as we could to see her, but when we arrived she was sleeping. She was technically alive but she had tubes in her arms connected to drips, and she wasn't herself at all.

The doctors were saying that they weren't sure if she was going to get better. We were still talking to her, though, and holding her hand. I said, 'We're here, Grandma. It's Marcus and Tash, just to let you know...' After a while, I felt her squeezing back, which I took as a promising sign, but a couple of days later she passed away. I was twenty-two. I had lost another grandparent, and I was devastated.

Me and my sisters with Grandma

I was sitting on a train to London recently and on the seat opposite was a little boy with his grandma. They were playing around, smiling at one another, and I was listening in on their conversation when it hit me. *Wow*, I thought, *I really miss Grandma. And Granny*. Even today I can be struck by those losses. Usually it happens when I least expect it, and it hurts.

I remember the last time Tash and I saw Grandma. It was that night in the hospital and we had looked at each other and made a decision, one that I'm so glad we made.

'Right, this might be the last moment we see her alive,' I said. 'Let's say our goodbyes – just in case.'

We squeezed her hand and told her how much we loved her and how amazing she was. It was horrible, but we knew we had to do it, and I learned at that moment that **YOU CAN'T PREDICT WHAT'S GOING TO HAPPEN IN LIFE.** You have to go with what comes your way. By that I mean, let nature take its course. If you need to release your emotions, don't be afraid to do so. If you need to talk about it with someone, do it – get the hurt and the worry off your chest. But if you don't want to talk about it, don't. You'll know what's right for you. And don't feel bad about the way you feel. Family loss is painful – it's important to look after yourself and the people around you.

IT'S OK TO BE SAD, TOO. My emotions were all over the place – everyone in the family felt the same way, but that was OK. We all knew it was fine to hurt. So, when someone passes away and you want to cry – do it. Try not to hold everything in because that can create tension, and it will eventually affect everything else around you. It might affect your job; it might affect your schoolwork; it might even affect your friendships and relationships. If you can get some of it out of your system through talking and crying, it will help in the long term.

'FAMILY LOSS IS PAINFUL - IT'S IMPORTANT TO LOOK AFTER YOURSELF AND THE PEOPLE AROUND YOU.'

Not that I understood this at first. Like a lot of people, I sometimes tried to hide my emotions away, particularly in tricky situations. It's always been that way, and when Grandma died I didn't cry at first, even though I was heartbroken. My sisters were in bits, though. Heidi sobbed her eyes out when she heard the news, whereas I didn't, and I remember questioning my reactions. I kept thinking, *This is probably the closest relative I've lost and I'm not crying. Am I strange emotionally? Am I a weirdo? Why am I not crying?* What I hadn't realised was that **DIFFERENT PEOPLE HURT IN DIFFERENT WAYS.**

But at the time I was so confused. I even mentioned it to Mum. 'Is it weird that I didn't cry?' I said shortly afterwards. 'I feel so sad, and she's been a major part of my life, so I feel really bad because I haven't cried.'

Mum was reassuring, as always. 'Just because you're not crying it doesn't mean you're not feeling it,' she said. 'You're just feeling it in a different way to your sisters. You don't have to cry to show anything. There are no rules to grieving.'

She was right, and I guess with all the emotions and grief flying around, it's important that you **DON'T FEEL GUILTY.** That was another emotion that was eating away at me, because at the time of Grandma's death, I hadn't been around as much, even though she was my last grandparent. There was college, and other things going on in my life. Realising that set me off to analysing our time together negatively. *Wow, did I see her enough?* I thought. *Did we do enough together?*

I got to the point where I had to get realistic. I thought, *Look, instead of focusing on all the bad stuff, I've got all of these amazing memories to concentrate on. I shouldn't think about the time she fell, or those moments in the hospital. Instead I should focus on the good times we had together.*

And there were plenty of them. Moments that I'll tell my own kids and grandkids about (when I have them, of course – there aren't any running around just yet). Those fond memories will never go away and I've since decided to celebrate her time with us instead. Grandma and Granny were huge parts of my life. They're gone, and it's hard to think of their loss, but I'm lucky to have had so many great times with them.

The final piece of advice I would give to anyone going through the heartbreak of a family loss is to **LIVE YOUR OWN LIFE**. That sounds like the hardest thing to do under the circumstances I know. And, yes, their passing will always be a thing, it will always come back, but it's important to keep going forwards. I remember our first family dinner after Grandma had died. We toasted her together, but it was a positive gesture. There were no wallowing speeches; it was done with a sense of moving on. Because that's what Grandma would have wanted. I promise you, that's what your loved one would want, too.

Use the person as an inspiration. If you're mourning and you feel depressed and unable to do anything, think about what they're doing, wherever you want to believe they are. If they were looking down on you in that moment, would they want you to be sad? I'm guessing they'd want you to be chasing your dreams and living your life to the full. Death is awful, and the pain is so huge, but you need to find some positives eventually, otherwise it will hold you back. And nobody wants that.

WHY PARENTS KNOW BEST

It's easy to believe that older people are the enemy when you're younger. It's easy to imagine that they don't really understand what you're going through, or that they don't get your personal issues and the crap you're having to deal with, especially when times are tough. The truth is, your mum, dad, even your grandparents, will have dealt with similar problems when they were living life as an almost-adult. They will have experienced bereavement, a break-up, maybe even the stress that comes with a serious illness. Sure, the world is a very different place now, but I bet they've experienced identical emotions to you at one stage or another.

I know my parents have, and for some strange reason I've always found it easy to talk to them about all kinds of stuff – from school issues and work stress to girls and relationships. Mum, in particular, has always made it really easy for me to talk about relationships, which I think is seriously important as a parent. She was always very open and easy to chat to. It helped that she knew me so well, of course, but whenever something was wrong in a relationship, or if I was having some kind of girl problem, she could always tell. Mum knew how to talk to me in a non-cringey way, and her advice nearly always helped me to resolve whatever issue I'd been freaking out over.

Even now, when something's wrong I can go and talk to Mum about it. If something's bothering me with work or a friend, I can call up Mum and she'll usually know the right thing to say. So far, she's prepared me for life: exams, relationships, stress. You name it, she's probably delivered a few words of wisdom on the subject, and ninety-nine per cent of the time she's been right, too. (Mum'll probably say that she has a hundred per cent record, but nobody's perfect, not even her. Though she's pretty close.)

The funny thing is I always feel that when Mum gives advice it's as if a higher power has spoken. She knows the answers to everything, and she'll usually have a story that relates to my own personal issue. It's the same with Dad. I'll tell him about some problem or other that's bothering me, and he'll tell me a funny or helpful tale from when he was younger. Thinking about it, I'm almost in a better relationship with my parents now because it seems as if we can talk

Me and Mum on holiday in Rhodes (Greece) July 2010

about anything. They don't treat me like a child and I've grown into an adult relationship with them. It's like we're equals in some respects.

The close-knit family at home – me, Mum, my stepdad and sisters – is quite special. We have this bond where we can talk about anything. There's a confidence between us that allows the whole family to be open and honest with each other, though I know that's probably quite an unusual thing, and not a lot of people feel comfortable in that environment.

That relaxed attitude and openness hasn't always been there, though. When I was younger, I thought of Mum and Dad as two older people. In my mind they had done very little with their lives, apart from raise me and my sisters – which I now realise to be a pretty massive achievement, along with all the other incredible things both of them have done. I figured that they had grown up in a sensible fashion; there was no way they would have done anything stupid or crazy as teenagers, not like me and my mates. The reality is very different, though. Chances are, my parents have done plenty of things that they wouldn't want to tell me about. Yours too, most probably. (Don't think too hard about it; you'll only gross yourself out.)

I know I'm lucky. Not everyone has parents that are as open, loving and supportive as mine. Even when Mum and Dad split up, both of them worked hard to raise the family in the best way possible. Life became very different when they divorced, for sure, but they still worked hard to help me follow my dreams.

My goal then was to become a professional basketball player. I was lucky that both of them were supportive of me, and they helped me to take a shot at it, even though life was unstable and frightening for them at the time. Whenever there were county trials or training sessions, Dad would drive me there. If there was a school match or a tournament, he would cheer me on from the sidelines. I think he must have given up nearly every weekend to help out during basketball season because there was always some match or other going on in places such as Southampton or London.

Mum made a similar sacrifice, though, because at the time, Heidi was working hard to be a footballer. While Dad was helping me to follow my ambitions, Mum was helping Heidi follow hers. They shared the responsibility during a time when life was hard for them. We both felt very supported and loved. That was always going to help us to progress in life, no matter what we did.

I'm not sure if I appreciated it then, though. When you're a teenager it's easy to think of your parents as the enemy. Inside you're grumpy and hormonal. You're discovering your sexuality, your passions and all the things in life that you want to be. You're unsure and frightened about who you are and where you're going, and there are so many changes taking place in your body and your brain that it's easy to become moody, even with your mum and dad.

Me and my Uncle Nigel at Disneyland Paris

Welcoming our little sister Heidi into the world

I know I was. Sometimes, when I was having a bad day, they could see my pain. They wanted to help. But my natural reaction, at first, was to slam the door on them – often literally. I soon learned to keep calm. In the end I listened to what they had to say, usually on whether or not I should do my homework. It didn't take me long to realise that they were the greatest allies I had, and I now know they helped to get me where I am today. They can be your launch pad to success, too.*

OK, here's how:

Problem: Uh-oh, the hormones are kicking in.

Solution: Parents are usually all over this trauma. They've been there, done that, got the embarrassing T-shirt. When you're growing up, there's a heck of a lot of awkward biological stuff going on. Periods. New body hair. Your voice goes crazy. Then the sex stuff starts. You're thinking, *I'm beginning to like girls*, or *I'm beginning to like guys*. You might even like both. Either way, your parents will have gone through something vaguely similar.

---

* That's your family, not mine. I mean, my family are great and I'm sure they'd like you, but that would be weird. Oh, and I know every family is different. You might be like me and have stepmums or stepdads. You might have grandparents rather than parents. Or you might have two mums or two dads. It doesn't really matter. If you love them and they love you, they can all be supportive in their own way.

My advice would be to go to Mum for most of this stuff, especially if you're a girl. Dads can be a little squeamish when it comes to bodily fluids and sexual organs. Of course, chat to the man of the house for questions such as, 'Should I shave this bit of face-fluff off, or can I look like Teen Wolf for a little while longer?' When I was younger, I sometimes found it a bit daunting when it came to discussing emotional stuff with Dad, because I felt like I had to impress him. With Mum I found it easier to open up and feel comfortable.

The thing is, everyone's different. It might be that in your family Dad is the best one to talk to about the emotional stuff, while your mum might be super-practical. Maybe a grandparent or a stepparent is the best person to discuss a tricky situation. Just pick the person you feel most relaxed with. And remember: they'll understand.

Problem: I've got a crush on my best mate.

Solution: When it came to discussing relationships, Mum ruled the roost in my family. She had experience in that department (though not too much experience, I hope – ugh!), and Dad really only wanted to talk about sports or mountain climbing. While both my parents will have experienced the first flushes of love, the insecurity of an unrequited crush and the desperate hurt of heartbreak, when it came to the issues of love, Mum knew best.

Again, I know that isn't the case for everyone. Your dad might be the best agony uncle in the world. And girls should always go to their dads for a guy's perspective – if they feel comfortable doing that. I know if I was confused about a girl I liked at college, I would ask Mum for her thoughts, because I figured, *Guys don't get girls, and girls don't get guys – I'll ask a woman.* That works both ways, so if you can, make the most of your dad's Yoda-like knowledge as well.

Problem: I have to go to a proper grown-up dinner.

Solution: Ask them over the dinner table. Get them to show you the right way to party in a mature manner. They'll definitely know how to order expertly in a restaurant. They might even be able to give you a few tips on picking a good wine. Chances are, one of them will buy you your first alcoholic drink, so all the skills you require to be a proper adult later on in life rest with Mum and Dad. (Just go easy on the booze, OK? You'll only confess some terribly embarrassing secret in the process.)

When it comes to the subject of fashion, try to steer clear, however. I know from experience that it can be a little awkward sometimes. For example, there have been times when I've shown up at my dad's house in a new top and he's eyed it up almost the second I've walked through the front door.

'So where did you get that, Marcus?' he'll say.

I'll tell him, and literally the next evening he'll be wearing exactly the same thing. It often looks ridiculous and I feel a bit stupid wearing the same clothes as my dad, so these days I pretend not to hear him when he asks.

Problem: Aaargh! I don't know what the hell I'm gonna do with my life!

Solution: You need all the help you can get on this one, so ask everyone you trust. Mum, Dad, sisters, brothers, uncles, aunties, the postman... OK, so maybe not the postman, but you get my drift.

When YouTube started to take off for me I went from ten followers to 10,000 and I was thinking about taking it more seriously. I was also thinking about going to university. I became confused. I asked Mum and my stepdad. I turned to Dad, too. It was a big life decision and I needed a shoulder or three to lean on. In the end Dad was great. He knew I wasn't making much from YouTube at the time and was unable to live off its earnings. He also knew it was a stab in the dark as a future career. But Dad could also tell that I was excited by the possibilities and he wanted me to chase my dream, so he sat down with me and together we worked out a business plan, plus a list of goals for the future. It really helped to focus my decision. I probably wouldn't be writing this book now without that meeting.

FRIENDS & FAMILY xx

PART 4

How to
GET THE LIFE
YOU WANT

How I came to be a YouTuber is a pretty crazy story. As a young kid I knew I didn't want to go down the traditional education route. I know it works really well for loads of people, but it just wasn't for me. I hated the fact that my life at school was being decided on coursework and exam results, and the thought of going through university, while picking up debts for tuition fees and living costs along the way, freaked me out. I was put off.

I'd always had a bit of a business head growing up and was often looking for different ways to make money, even when I was a little kid. When I was about twelve years old I went around the house finding random things to put on eBay, like Pokémon cards and Game Boy stuff. I later sold my old drum kit for £200. But I became even more creative as I got older. Like the time when I was fourteen and my mate Dave told me his brother had sold gig tickets on eBay for twice the cost price. That excited me. I liked the idea and thought I'd give it a go.

Wow, I thought, *I can make so much money from this!*

I scanned the gig-listing websites online and I noticed that George Michael (one for the mums out there) had just announced a big show in London, so I convinced Dad to lend me some cash.

'Reckon I can borrow fifty quid to buy some tickets, please?' I said. 'George Michael's coming to Wembley; it's going to be huge and I know I can sell my tickets for double the price, easily. You'll get fifty quid back straight away, and I'll make fifty quid profit.'

Luckily he agreed, and within days my tickets were going up in value – £50 to £70, and then £90. The experience gave me a real sense of money-making; I got a lot of satisfaction. It also opened me up to the idea of (slightly dodgy) business entrepreneurship, rather than the traditional educational system, which was viewed as the only way of becoming successful at my school. (The lawyer has told me this can be illegal now, so don't try it yourself. Sorry!)

Looking well chuffed on my first day back at school after the summer holidays

Then there were the heavy decisions that I was constantly being asked to make in my educational experience, usually during what felt like the worst possible moments in life. When I was fourteen, for example, my GCSE options came around. I was sporty and creative as a kid. I wanted to do PE, Music and Drama because I was passionate about those subjects. But the exam board restricted me to only one. They limited my 'expressive' options, as they did for all kids. The education system wanted me to focus on subjects across the board, like History and languages. It was a real nightmare.

Great, I thought. *You've shot down two of my three dreams in one swoop and I have to pick one. Talk about pressure.*

As if that wasn't bad enough, I had so much other stuff going on in my head, such as discovering girls, new body hair, a changing voice and all the other crazy hormonal challenges that came with being a moody teenager. There were also massive expectations pushing down on me from my parents and teachers at school. I felt constantly squeezed to make the right decisions, to hit the right grades. Making mistakes and learning from them didn't seem to be an option.

"I FELT CONSTANTLY SQUEEZED TO MAKE THE RIGHT DECISIONS, TO HIT THE RIGHT GRADES"

I didn't feel ready. I was being asked to make adult choices when I was only a kid, and I quickly understood why so many people become tense in those complicated moments. It felt like a massive headache, one that was set to change my life forever (or so I was led to believe) and there wasn't a great deal of advice or support to lead me along the way. It must be even worse for teenagers with other stressful dilemmas on their plate, like coming to terms with their sexuality or dealing with depression.

Looking back, I felt constantly disorientated at school and college. I was forever losing sight of what I wanted to be, whether that was an accountant, a musician, an actor or a basketball player. (I know. Random, right?) I was a pretty good ball player and I'd considered getting a scholarship to an American college for a while, which is where you get to move to the States on a special programme if you have the right grades. Once there, I'd get to play basketball and have a proper education. What a result that would have been.

That idea later fell away when I tried to pursue a more traditional work route into accountancy, though I'd really only been pulled into it because pretty much every family member – Mum, Dad, both my uncles – were qualified accountants. While I was at college Dad had told me that I could join his friend's firm when I'd finished, rather than going to uni and studying for a degree. I'd get paid and I could do my professional exams at the same time.

"A TECHNOLOGICAL REVOLUTION WAS KICKING OFF. I HAD DISCOVERED YouTUBE AND VLOGGING"

'You'll get a salary to learn,' he said, which sounded like a better idea than actually paying for an education myself.

But something else was taking shape that would change my life forever. A technological revolution was kicking off. I had discovered YouTube and vlogging, and the exciting possibilities that came with it were blowing me away.

These days YouTube is obviously a huge deal; it's one of the biggest sites and apps online, and it's probably why you're reading my book. Over a billion people visit it every month – that's a seventh of the world's population – and, at the time of writing, 300 hours of material are uploaded on the site every minute. The numbers are mind-bending. But back in the day, when I first started uploading videos in 2006, it was a very different place.

I was fourteen, and there were probably only a handful of videos on YouTube. I followed vloggers called Charlieissocoollike, Nigahiga and Shane Dawson. They really inspired me to be creative and to upload material, so I started putting up music videos from around the web that were only available in the UK for kicks. I would find footage of bands I really liked, and I'd stick it on YouTube. I was also piecing together sports-highlights packages and uploading them. It was amateur stuff, and I was forever getting hassled by various media companies over copyright issues, but it was fun.

It was successful, too. Some videos racked up 14 million views, which would still be considered amazing now. Back then that number was unbelievable. One basketball video pulled in 100,000 views, which gave me a huge rush; a music video I'd illegally streamed drew in 250,000 hits. These were big numbers, but the funny thing was my mates thought I was a bit sad.

Screenshot from my first YouTube video on my channel – January 2010

'Dude, what are you doing?' they'd say at school. 'Putting up other people's work is so lame.'

I knew it could have been dodgy, legally, and I certainly wouldn't advise it now. But I could see potential online. I was drawing in thousands of views for random things I was uploading. I set up a channel of my own called MarcusBrapZap (I've no idea where that came from) and uploaded more covers. Then one day, out of the blue, a guy offered to pay me if I annotated my videos with his advertising links. I'd put them on my page, people would click on them, which would then upload one of his websites, though it was nothing too dodge, I'd like to point out. In return he'd pay me a monthly fee. At first I was suspicious. I had no idea what it all meant, but I went for it, and before long money was rolling into my PayPal account.

Yeah! I'm sixteen, making money from my videos! I thought. *Pretty cool!*

My parents were totally confused by it all. Deep down I think I was, too. I was turned on to making my own videos soon after when people started commenting on the profile photo on my channel. They wanted to know what I looked like for real. They wanted to see the person behind the photo, so one day I caved in and did a Q & A, which felt weird, a bit awkward, but people seemed to like it. Loads of positive comments appeared under the video, and a lot of them were telling me to start a new channel. So, inspired, I set up Marcus Butler TV.

I started mucking around. I made videos where I ranted about issues, such as friend-grabbing groups on Facebook. You know the kind of thing: people saying, 'Oh, I'll turn myself into Voldemort from Harry Potter if I get fifty new friends...' Proper lame stuff. My set-up was really basic; I had a crappy camera on top of my computer, which wobbled off sometimes, falling to the floor. People could also see my messy bedroom in the background. But as I moaned and took the p*** out of different issues, the positive comments kept rolling in.

I loved it. I was having fun. A lot of the other guys on YouTube were already up and running by then. People like Alfie Deyes had started around six months before me. Tyler Oakley was doing his stuff. The only person who wasn't around then was Joe Sugg. Me and Alfie met up after a couple of months of being into it, because we both lived in Brighton. We were friends a year and a half before meeting anyone else, and we'd decided to hang out and make videos after chatting to one another on our pages.

My first-ever display picture for my YouTube channel (what was I thinking!)

Online, I upped my game. I started taking the mickey out of *myself*. I did the FML Smoothie Challenge, a disgusting task where I went into the kitchen and put as much random stuff into a blender as I could find. I grabbed orange juice, raw eggs, mustard and ketchup. I mixed it up in a blender and gulped down the whole lot in one go without vomming. Gross. Don't try this at home! It was all really stupid and just something I was doing for fun really, but some of my videos were getting 30,000 views. It was insane.

Screenshot from my FML smoothie challenge video. Rank.

Around this time I applied for a YouTube Partnership. That might sound like a huge deal, but it just meant that I could make some extra money from the page, and with only 700 subscribers I was definitely expecting rejection. But one day, while I was in a PE class, YouTube contacted me with an acceptance email. They were asking if I'd like to be one of their partners. Loads of people had been signed up at that time, not that I knew, and I was so excited. When I received their email I was on top of the world; I thought, *How cool is this? I'm going to get paid for doing something I love.* I was so excited and almost ready to quit my part-time job.

In reality, I wasn't getting anywhere near enough to give up the day job. Still, I was having fun. After I'd hit 7,000 subscribers, I went travelling with my best friend, Max. We had just left college and were about to start new lives, so we decided to go to Australia for two months. At the time I was about to begin working at Dad's friend's accountancy firm. I was making new videos every week, but it was still a fun thing rather than a serious concern, which was probably why I didn't think about taking a laptop away with me. I had no idea just how much impact my posts had been making until I started checking my channel. Every time I went to an internet cafe, I was getting messages from people wanting to know where I'd been. It wasn't loads, but enough to make me reconsider what I was doing.

Wow, I thought. *They're saying they miss me and my videos. This isn't cool having two months off and not doing anything. I need to get back in front of the camera...*

When I got home, I knew I had to make more of my YouTube ambitions.

Feeling like we've just conquered the world after climbing a rock in the outback of Australia

Me and Max exploring the Grampians National Park in Australia

Something big was happening online – the accountancy work was secondary in my head – so at every opportunity I made vlogs or messed around with visual effects on my laptop. Incredibly I later won a YouTube competition called Next Up – an event that promoted the work of young YouTube creatives, and they were looking for the next '25 Online Stars' from across Europe. I scooped €20,000 for a crazy freeze-frame video where I put together loads of different visual effects I had taught myself.

It was mad. In the end I decided to give up on accountancy – it wasn't for me. I got a job with a software firm and planned to travel the US with Niomi the following year. For a little while I'd considered going against all those gut feelings about my suitability for higher education. I'd got myself accepted into the University of the West of England, and I was going to take the debt head on and study for a degree in Business and Marketing.

But my thoughts on that were changing, too. I had won all this money, my YouTube channel had started picking up thousands more subscribers, and I was at the forefront of an internet phenomenon. Suddenly I had found a new purpose, and without the need for exams, revision or tuition fees. I was going to be a YouTuber. Talk about getting a lucky break.

HOW TO GET THE LIFE YOU WANT
(AND HANDLE PRESSURE ALONG THE WAY)

Look, I know what you're thinking. You're probably reading this, scratching your head, saying, 'Marcus, it's all right for you, stumbling into YouTube success, winning €20,000 competitions along the way. Like that's ever going to happen to me.'

Trust me, I know I'm lucky. I know I was in the right place at the right time and I've since realised that my stroke of good fortune doesn't happen every day. But the point I'm trying to make here is that I got to where I am today by not freaking out about school, exams or college too much. I located a dream target and I went for it, and I didn't need qualifications or a university education to achieve it.

Before we go any further, I understand that for a lot of people qualifications *are* important. If you want to be a doctor or a lawyer, for example, you'll need to pass the big exams. Being a student can also be one of the most pivotal and exciting times of your life. I remember going to the University of West England to stay with Niomi. She had an amazing time there and met loads of friends that she will stay close to for ever. She also got the education she wanted to drive herself forwards in life. Most of my mates from our group of friends went, too.

If that's the life choice for you, then go for it. You'll need to study hard and make some serious grades, but it'll be worth it. However, for others – people like me – it's important to realise that exams aren't the be all and end all, no matter what your teachers might say. And for those of you reading this who are having to take exams to achieve their life goals, remember this: if you fail them, you can always take them again.

I guess that's important to remember when dealing with the one thing everyone has to handle in their life – pressure. It hits us all, no matter who we are, or what we want to achieve. Pressure to succeed. Pressure to conform to what your school wants you to achieve. Pressure to get the right grades. Pressure to follow a certain road map to success. Pressure to be happy. Pressure to fit in with your peers. These are just some of the issues that teachers or lecturers don't always help you to manage at school or uni.

'FOR THOSE OF YOU READING THIS WHO ARE HAVING TO TAKE EXAMS TO ACHIEVE THEIR LIFE GOALS, REMEMBER THIS: IF YOU FAIL THEM, YOU CAN ALWAYS TAKE THEM AGAIN.'

I've experienced various pressures throughout my life so far, and I want to help you to handle the times where pressure is heavy, because although it feels lonely, everyone goes through it. And if you can navigate the stress, you've got a greater chance of getting the life you want while following your dreams through to the end.

LESSON # |
CHILL OUT

LESSON #1: CHILL OUT

That would be the advice I'd give to my younger self. Back in the day, I had teachers constantly putting pressure on me to pass exams. To ace essays. The consequences for failure, I was told, were huge. I remember we even had days in college where we learned how to fill in our university application forms. Think about it: a big bunch of kids, all of them different, all of them with unique hopes and personalities being squeezed through the exact same university application system. How does that work?

I hated it. And because I wasn't used to handling pressure, when it hit me it was hard to nail down. It spun me out a little. I was feeling a load of strange emotions, but I didn't know why. Things only got better once I'd pinpointed the cause of my stress, which was the pressure to go to university – and it was coming from other people not me.

For you, the source of your anxiety might be something else, but the key thing I recognised was that once I understood the cause of my issue, I could deal with it. Was I stressing myself out too much? Was it all caused by other people?

Once I worked out what was bothering me, I talked to someone about it, in this case my parents. I told them I wanted to make a go of YouTube, that I didn't think university life was for me. I don't think they really understood what YouTube was at first, but they could see I was getting positive attention. They saw that I was passionate about it, and so they supported me. I was very lucky in that respect.

'I TOLD THEM I WANTED TO MAKE A GO OF YouTube, THAT I DIDN'T THINK UNIVERSITY LIFE WAS FOR ME.'

But talking helped to ease the pressure. I was getting stressed out about what would happen if I didn't go to university. I worried my life might not work out in a way that I wanted. Once I got it off my chest, I felt better. I think too many people allow pressure to build up inside them. Eventually they explode because it gets too much for them to handle. So get it out through talking before you fall into an unsettled state of mind.

Here's a funny story about pressure and how it can freak me out. There was an upcoming inter-house swimming event at my school and I was one of the very few people in my house who could make it up and down the length of a pool without drowning. Because I was fairly good in other sports, people assumed that I'd be a good swimmer, too, even though I was probably just average. So, one afternoon, the teacher organising the event approached me after a lesson.

'Marcus,' he said. 'I hear you can do the hundred-metre medley. Fancy racing in the gala?'
'Well, sir, I've never swum anything like butterfly, but I can do the front crawl.'
'Perfect!' he said. 'You're in! Oh, by the way, one of your competitors swims for England.'

My stomach sank. *Cool, no big deal then*, I thought. *Maybe I'll pull a sickie that week.*

When the day of the competition came around, I had honestly forgotten about the race, and I'd left my swimming kit at home. That wasn't going to stop it happening, though. From thin air, a tight pair of Speedos appeared. They had probably been dragged from lost property, thrown away by some poor kid out of embarrassment most likely. I was thirteen and going through puberty. Standing up in front of the whole school in a little pair of unwashed swimming trunks on a freezing-cold day was not going to enhance my rep as some kind of 'player'. It was awful.

'STANDING UP IN FRONT OF THE WHOLE SCHOOL IN A LITTLE PAIR OF UNWASHED SWIMMING TRUNKS ON A FREEZING-COLD DAY.'

Right, everyone's watching me, I thought, as I got to the pool. *I'm up against someone who swims for England and I'm the worst swimmer out of all these kids. Plus I'm in these ridiculously tight trunks that have been worn by someone else. Aaaaaagh!*

I wanted to get out of there – and fast. I felt sick, scared and tense. I would have done anything for the ground to have swallowed me whole. It was the kind of awful moment that still gives me nightmares today, and I wouldn't have wished it on my worst enemy. Unsurprisingly I came last, and I didn't live it down for ages.

In hindsight, I should have been strong enough to explain my concerns to the teacher. If I'd told him that I wasn't good enough to compete, I wouldn't have got myself into that embarrassing mess in the first place. And I definitely wouldn't have had to stand in front of the whole school while wearing the worst swimming trunks in history.

LESSON #2:
IT'S OK TO DREAM

The educational system is great for people who want to be an accountant, or an architect, or a surgeon. But what if you want to be something a bit more creative or vocational, like a painter, or a photographer, or a plumber?

I've learned that it's easy to fall into the trap of thinking negatively about your dreams. Something like, *I love acting, and I'm great at it, but no one notices me. I don't get any educational rewards for it, and people are saying it's not a proper job. So how am I meant to succeed in life?*

Resignation follows soon after. You think that maybe it's not the path for you. There's pressure to follow a more traditional educational route – Maths, say – and suddenly that more exciting dream has gone, maybe for ever.

When I was younger I wish there had been an accessible voice, a friend or family member who could have told me, 'Look, there are other options. Life isn't just about the things you're being told by teachers. There are other ways of living. It's not all about school, getting to university, getting that career. You're allowed to work out what makes you happy.' Had I known that, I would have been a lot less worked up.

I've also learned that it's all very well doing a job because the money is good, but what really matters is happiness. So don't rush into your career and educational choices. Look at different ways of fulfilling your dreams and don't be scared to try new things while you're young. You have plenty of time. Most importantly, believe in your abilities. That way you're giving yourself the best shot of getting the life you really want.

LESSON #3: YOU'LL ALWAYS HAVE PRESSURE

That's the truth. There's always some sort of stress going on: at work, home, school, with friends or family. It's part of life, but it's not always bad. It can spur you on to get things done. If you can manage it properly, you can hit deadlines and impress your boss. You can surpass personal goals and improve your life.

When Alfie and I were first starting our YouTube channels and things were getting serious, Jamie Oliver invited us to work with him on a video. Alfie and I had been mates for a while. We'd done plenty of stuff together on our channels, and we'd been trying to break a load of world records for the Guinness World Records YouTube channel. Jamie reckoned that his mentor, the Italian chef, Gennaro Contaldo, could break the figure for the number of fresh ravioli parcels made in a minute, which was some challenge.

It was our job to present the attempt on video and our reaction, when we were asked, was crazy. We were both thinking, *Wow, this could be cool, but, man, this is nerve-wracking!* We knew that Jamie was a monumental figure on TV and that he could really help our online presence, but it was hard not to build up the situation in our heads. What if I fluffed my lines? What if I swore? It was exciting but

Me, Alfie and Jamie Oliver. First time we met and cooked with him.

really scary. In the end I realised we both had to relax, to not overthink the stress involved and take every moment as it came.

We both travelled to Jamie Oliver's studio in London and met all of his team, including Gennaro, but there was no sign of the man himself. What a drama, though! No joke, there were about forty members of the crew running around the place. Alfie and me were pretty lo-fi at the time: we were one-man shows, literally, with our laptops and cameras, so to see this huge team carrying lights and running cables through the studio was a mad experience.

It was only when we were miked up for the first time that the director explained what would be happening.

'Right,' he said. 'Just to give you the lowdown, Jamie's gonna come in soon. When he does, boom! You guys run the show. It's your thing. Cool?'

We didn't know what to do, but from the minute Jamie walked in everything was fine.

'What's going on, boys?' he shouted as he rocked up.

It was a great ice-breaker. Suddenly the nerves were forgotten. We were running on adrenalin, working with the pressure. It sharpened my mind and helped me to perform better. It helped Gennaro, too. He smashed the record, nailing twenty-four ravioli in a minute.

LESSON #4: MESSING UP ISN'T THE END

In fact, if you don't let the failure dissuade you from what it is you're trying to achieve, it's probably just the beginning of something new. Don't believe me? Look at most of the successful business people in the world: none of them have got to where they are without making mistakes. Simon Cowell, Richard Branson, Alan Sugar, Peter Jones: I've read their autobiographies and none of them were put off by the fear of making mistakes.

Whenever they were knocked down, they didn't stay disheartened for too long. They got straight back up again, learned from their errors and continued on their quest for success. You can do that, too. If you have a goal, the determination to succeed, willpower and an understanding there will be setbacks along the way, nothing can stand in your path.

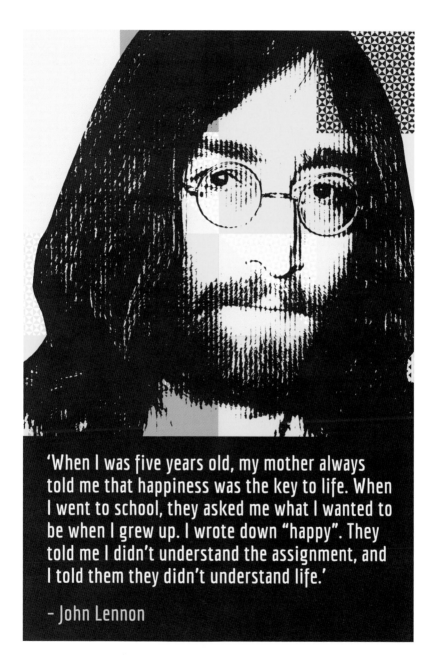

'When I was five years old, my mother always told me that happiness was the key to life. When I went to school, they asked me what I wanted to be when I grew up. I wrote down "happy". They told me I didn't understand the assignment, and I told them they didn't understand life.'

– John Lennon

EXAM JITTERS: THE CURE

When it came to exams I was never the best. I rarely put all my focus into nailing them, and revision was always a bore to me. If ever Niomi and me were studying in the school library together, I'd always be making excuses to duck out of the work. At any moment I might pop off to get us some snacks or drinks, or I'd make phone calls outside, or watch movies on my phone. Anything to avoid doing the practical stuff. I used to distract her so much when we were 'revising'. I'd even draw pictures all over her work notes. She'd always laugh, but I was probably a bad influence.

That was both good and bad. Good because I never stressed myself out over exams. (Sure, I'd get a little nervous, but I'd rarely work myself up into a state.) Bad because my lack of focus sometimes meant that I'd take my eye off the ball altogether.

One time while I was at college, I was waiting to leave the house for an end-of-year Pyschology exam. I had ten minutes until the test started, but I only lived a couple of minutes away, so I flipped on the TV. My attitude was, *Oh, I'm all right, I can drive there and make it in time.* I left everything until the last minute and, typically, I hadn't planned for my day. When the time finally came to leave, I realised my pencil case wasn't organised, and I was running around, grabbing my pens in a panic. Once I'd got to college I couldn't find a parking space. I was driving down the road screaming and yelling at myself; I was so annoyed.

I was only five minutes late in the end, but when I walked into the sports hall where the exam was taking place, everyone turned round to look at me. I must have looked a mess. I was sweating and panting, but at least I'd learned a valuable lesson: always be prepared for an exam, right down to the last detail.

'ALWAYS BE PREPARED FOR AN EXAM, RIGHT DOWN TO THE LAST DETAIL.'

Make sure you have the correct equipment. Make sure you know where you're going. Oh, and make sure you know what exam you're taking.

If ever I was to take a test again – and I really hope I don't have to – I'd prepare in a thorough way. Well, if I've not left my revision to the last minute, of course. Which I strongly suggest you don't do. But if I was prepared on **THE DAY BEFORE**, I'd relax. Maybe I'd look at a checklist of reminders and revision bullet points for the exam, but beyond that there's really no point. If the relevant info isn't in my head twenty-four hours before a test, then it's never going to get there. Rather than revising, I'd exercise, hang out with friends or go into town to see a movie. Anything to take my mind off the next day.

THE NIGHT BEFORE: I'd watch another film, or box set, but nothing too stressful. Watching a mind-bending movie or something really depressing is not a good idea. But fun, easy viewing like *Scrubs*, *Friends*, *How I Met Your Mother* or *The Big Bang Theory* are always good for a laugh. Once I'm chilled, I'd spend ten minutes reading through my notes as a final refresher.

I always find it's good to listen to something relaxing the night before an exam, whether that's a chill-out soundtrack, classical or some acoustic stuff. It sets me into a calm rhythm. Whenever I'm working, I'll often find a laid-back playlist on Spotify and have it in the background. If I need to get stuff done, I'll stick music on – that's always helped to focus me in the past.

'IT'S GOOD TO LISTEN TO SOMETHING RELAXING THE NIGHT BEFORE AN EXAM, WHETHER THAT'S A CHILL-OUT SOUNDTRACK, CLASSICAL OR SOME ACOUSTIC STUFF.'

ON THE DAY: I've found that high-pressure situations are easier to deal with if I accept the nerves first. I try to use them rather than fight them – the butterflies help me to focus. It's also worth remembering that everyone else will be stressed, so never feel like you're freaking out on your own in an exam situation. Unless it's a driving test, in which case: 'Aaaaaargh!!!'

Once the teacher has uttered those cringey words 'Three–two–one… you may begin…' my advice would be to shut everyone else out around you, especially the keen kid on the next table who's written 500 words in the first ten minutes. Play your own game. If you're thinking, *Crap! She's written so much! I need to get more down…* just imagine they've written a load of total gibberish.

AFTERWARDS: Don't get involved in the post-exam analysis. Everyone puts themselves through it, almost from the minute the papers have been handed in, and it's always torture. If someone asks you what you scribbled down for the last question to your summer finals, just say: 'It's done. I've got three months to relax and party. I'm going to worry about the paper once my results are in.'

Easier said than done, I know, but it'll save you a whole load of stress. You should be celebrating, not over-analysing any potential mistakes. Don't throw away your revision notes, though. Just in case...

'You can only do so much, and then you're at the mercy of fortune.'
– Woody Allen

GETTING A REAL JOB

I didn't want to get a part-time job when I was at college. I was seventeen when Mum first said to me, 'Marcus, you need to earn some money for yourself.' She was right. I wasn't receiving a grant for my education, and although Dad was giving me £200 a month to support myself, I was paying rent at home. At the time, I thought it was a pretty strange request as none of my friends were doing that with their parents. Though, looking back, those bills gave me an understanding of how important it was to pay something important every month. Still, my allowance wasn't enough, especially as most of my friends were working. I could see they were able to afford nice clothes, nights out and fun stuff, whereas I was limited with my cash flow.

In the end I bit the bullet. *Right*, I thought, *I'm getting a job!* I printed off several CVs and walked through the Churchill Square shopping centre in Brighton, dropping them off into all the shops – Debenhams, Hollister, Next and River Island. After a couple of weeks, Next called me up. They wanted me to attend a group interview and I was really excited. *Sick! Someone actually wants me! And I might get some free clothes as well...*

I had no experience of interviews at all back then. We used to do a thing at college called 'ice-breakers'. Whenever a new class started up, everyone introduced themselves to the people sitting nearby. I hated it – I used to cringe inside – and I had the same awkward feeling about my interview with Next.

It went well, though. I was asked back for a trial day, to see if I could cut it in the high-flying world of affordable fashion, and talk about a baptism of fire! There was a heatwave that day and our air conditioning had broken down. It felt like it was a hundred degrees in the building. Staff members were walking around complaining. I kept my mouth shut and stuck to my job, which was to guard the open fire escape, making sure some air could rush in, while stopping any potential shoplifters from legging it out the back with a bag of ties.

I got the job in the end, but I can still remember the nerves all too well. It was a nightmare, and not too dissimilar to being on *The Apprentice*, I'd imagine, which I watched religiously every week back then. (I looked into getting on the show, but according to the terms and conditions I was too young.) What the experience (and Lord Sugar) taught me was that it wasn't enough to simply write a good CV. Getting a job often begins with seeing the advert, and it ends when you close the door behind you after an interview, but there are more than a few pitfalls along the way.

GO FOR IT

Always be realistic. If you're a great taxi driver, the next step isn't necessarily to be a Ferrari test car driver. Having said that, it's always worth aiming a little higher, just in case you get through the interview stages with flying colours. You might unexpectedly land a super-cool gig.

The flip side of this situation is if you aim a little lower – a job where you're slightly overqualified, for example – then you're more than likely going to be the best candidate, giving you the opportunity to get the job, make the position your own and work your way up from there.

GET YOUR CV RIGHT

I wrote a CV back in the day, but it was put together with a lot of help from my sister. I basically copied several things that she'd written on hers. I made claims to being 'diligent' and 'works great as an individual as well as in teams'. But I also learned to never write 'using Facebook' in the 'Hobbies and Interests' section. A candidate who does that can look unimaginative, and maybe a bit of a slacker. Unless, of course, your job is online-media-based. In that case you're all right (though don't quote me on that). It also doesn't go down well if you write 'socialising'. It's a bit like saying 'I love going down the pub.'

'ORGANISATION, DILIGENCE AND TIME MANAGEMENT.'

Since those days, I've learned that a CV has to be versatile – you might even need to write a slightly different CV for every application you do. Look at the job you're going for and tailor your words accordingly. If the role requires leadership skills, say, list the things you've done in the past that needed you to take charge. Likewise, organisation, diligence and time-management. Then make sure the CV is a couple of pages long with **ABSOLUTELY NO SPELLING OR GRAMMATICAL ERRORS** – rite?

NO FIBS

Because you will get caught out. Especially if you've claimed to be a stuntman in your spare time.

LOOK SMART

This should go without saying, but make sure you look snappy during your interview, even if the company representative you're meeting is laid-back and cool. Dress well. Shower. Clean your fingernails. And make sure you knock on the door before entering for your interview. Then

Dress well. Shower. Clean your fingernails.

smile and firmly shake the hand of the person you're meeting (but don't break their knuckles). First impressions are always important.

THINGS TO SAY

- During the interview: I'd really like to work for your company.
- If you get the job: Thank you. (Well, obviously.)
- If you don't get the job: Thank you for taking the time to meet me. If another opportunity comes up, please do consider me.

Trust me, people remember good manners because they're so rare these days.

FIVE WAYS TO ORGANISE YOUR SUPER-BUSY LIFE

I'm not really disorganised, but I'm not the most time-efficient of people either. I used to leave things to the last minute, like packing my bags for school or work. Luckily I've got a lot better at arranging my life, as you'll soon find out.

Back in the day, though, my little sister, Heidi, was the most organised person I knew. She would get home from school, unpack her stuff and repack it for the next day. My attitude? Get home, throw my bag on the floor, and then inevitably wake up the next morning in a blind panic.

So, what have I got today? I'd think. *Oh, yeah, Maths, PE, double Science... Aaaagh! Where is everything? Mum!*

I know. Annoying.

I've got better now. I'm very good with timings, and I don't like being late. Before meetings I'll always watch the clock and I like to ready myself, because when I'm motivated I'm super-organised. If I have a goal to achieve I'll rearrange my life to hit that target. Don't get me wrong, I have my moments of chaos, running around in a rush to make a meeting, grabbing things as I fly out of the front door, and generally stressing myself out. But for the most part I'm pretty nailed on in terms of sorting my life.

Want to know how I made the switch? Well, follow these steps and you'll be ruling the day like the Queen.

1 ▶ SET GOALS

First up, the basics: listing goals, big or small. I use notes in my phone to organise myself. If ever I'm lacking in motivation, or feeling a bit disorganised, I'll flip back to my phone, check my notes and refocus. It's a big help, and these goals fall into two categories:

#1 YEARLY TARGETS

In December, just before News Year's Eve, I'll write a list of what I want to achieve during the following year. It's a 'blue sky' manifesto – a load of targets I'd like to hit in an ideal world. So at the end of 2014, for example, I typed in the following:

THE MARCUS LIST, 2015

1. Become a boss at Minecraft
2. Laugh more
3. Launch a new business
4. Move to London or LA
5. Hit 3 million subscribers
6. Travel to a different country
7. Make another rap song
8. Write an award-winning, bestselling book (still hoping for this)

As you can see, the goals in my phone aren't just work-related. There are some life goals as well, and whenever I'm lacking in motivation I'll look back at them. Right off the bat I'll know whether I'm sticking to my aims or not. It'll get me back on track if I'm drifting. Also, with a yearly list, I have clear targets. Even though I might forget some of them (I just had to check my phone to recall all of those points), subconsciously they're burned onto the back of my brain.

It's amazing. Often I'll find that when I go back at the end of the year, I've actually made most of my targets. I might have even surpassed my expectations. That's the perfect endgame.

#2 DAILY TARGETS

I've started doing this more recently, and it helps big time. Whenever I have a lot to do, I find that writing a checklist of targets in the morning sets me up for the day. It's like a pathway to a successful twenty-four hours. It's not the same for everyone, I know. Some people will wake up and just know what they have to do, and when. My mum and is like that. She's organised. Everything is filed neatly in her head. Heidi's the same.

Tash and I are different. I need to visualise what I have to do in order to execute it properly,

so I'll have little sticky notes pinned to my desk or laptop. Every morning I'll write out my list of daily tasks. Then I'll cross through things when I've completed them in a super-satisfying adrenalin rush of smugness. Done, done, *done*!

2 ▸ STICK TO ONE THING

Don't believe the hype! Multitasking doesn't lead to hyper-productivity. In fact, it actually has the opposite effect. I was recently reading a science study that claimed multitasking creates the illusion of achievement: it *feels* like you're doing loads, but what's actually happening is that you're doing more stuff, only less efficiently. And taking your eye off the ball only causes more work for you in the long run because you won't have completed the ten tasks you were doing (at once) as well as you should have.

I'm terrible for that. I like starting new things. I'll have my list and I'll buzz off the fact I'm starting a new task. Then halfway through I find I'm starting something else. I'll end up doing half my list at once and everything becomes a jumble. At the end of a day I'm often left wondering, *Er, I've finished some stuff, but I haven't done nearly as much as I would have liked, and the stuff I've done isn't as good as I had hoped it would be...*

So my advice is this: stick to one thing as much as possible. Get in the zone and focus. Once you've nailed it, move on to the next target.

⟨✖⟩ LIFE HACK!

Set your passwords to match your goals. With email accounts, work log-ins, Facebook details, decide on something that reflects one of your bigger aims, for example: 'EATHEALTHY2015' or 'UNIVERSITY2016'. It will reinforce your targets every day without you thinking about it too hard.

3 ► PUT THINGS AWAY

Seriously! Stop leaving a trail of destruction around the house or office, and find a home for every single item you own. (Those were my mum's famous words to me while growing up.) It sounds obvious, but so few people do it and it leads to much less chaos. Think about it: how many times have you been leaving the house in a rush, unable to find your phone, headphones or keys? A lot, I'd imagine.

I know, because until recently I was quite messy. I'd leave jumpers lying about the house, or paperwork. Don't get me wrong, I'm big on cleanliness, and if ever a kitchen top is dirty, I'm all over it like Mr Muscle. But I've been disorganised in the past, and I've since found that by finding a home for everything – and I mean, *everything* – I can have a go-to spot whenever I'm getting ready in a blur.

Phone? Check. Headphones? Check. Car keys? Check.

It's a little bit boring, but try it. It'll make you double efficient in times of stress. Though I should really tattoo this to my own arm because I don't always stick to my own advice.

4 ▶ WAKE UP EARLY

I'm lucky. I don't *have* to wake up; I don't have to commute to college, school or work and be at my desk at 9 a.m. If I wanted to, I could stay in bed all morning, but I always feel guilty because the day is getting wasted.

Instead I like to be up early because I feel like I'm more motivated to get my tasks done if I'm awake, showered and fed when the working day starts, even if my jobs for the day are house chores. It also means I have more time to complete the things I want to get done.

5 ▶ LEARN YOUR ALARM CLOCK ACTION PLAN

The alarm goes off, and what do you do? Roll out of bed and cruise through the morning, killing it at breakfast, ruling the bathroom in style, and power dressing like a boss before leaving the house ahead of time? Or do you bundle around in a daze, bleary-eyed and ineffective?

If it's the latter, then you clearly need to work on your morning routine to the minute. By that I mean record the time it takes for you to get your game face on and grab the day by the scruff of the neck. If you can figure out roughly how many minutes you need to set yourself up in the morning, you'll never be late out of the door again.

Here's my timetable...

- Shower, get ready, do hair – 20 mins
- Breakfast (porridge, coffee) – 20 mins, including washing-up
- Getting bag together – 10 mins
- Emails, YouTube, etc. – 20 mins
- General faffing – 5 mins (I love a general faff!)

Total: one hour, 15 mins. But if I'm in a real rush, I can be showered, dressed and fed within half an hour.

Ohhh yeahhhhh!

✖ LIFE HACK!

Never waste a coffee buzz. You'll have a rush of focus after a cup, so do your emails, finalise your important paperwork, and get your day planned. You'll find the caffeine energy will make you productive. Those emails will be full of positivity, too. Just don't drink too much oreveryonewillthinkyou'reabitweirdbecauseyou'retalkinggibberish. Got it?

THE MARCUS BUTLER
RANDOM-POSITIVE-THOUGHT GENERATOR

I like the idea of having a healthy mind as much as I love having a healthy body.
So when Niomi came to me with a cool idea about setting my head right from
the minute I wake in the morning, I was interested. The general idea is that you
should think of three really positive things as soon as your eyes open and you
start to stir in bed. It is a sure-fire way of kicking your day into action from
the get-go.

**'We both have to lay there for a few minutes,' she said. 'In that time we have
to think three positive thoughts. It could be things that you're thankful for in
life, or three things you want to achieve in twenty-four hours, or the week,
or even in the year. It's three positive ideas to set you up for the day.'**

I've got to admit, the first time was a bit odd. We were both lying there with our
eyes closed, not saying anything. It was almost impossible not to laugh at first. In
the end I said, 'OK, let's do it properly!' And we spent a few minutes in silence,
thinking uplifting thoughts. I went over the things I was grateful for in my life –
my YouTube followers, Niomi and my family. Almost immediately, my mood felt
strong. I was happy, energised and focused.

I know it sounds a bit of a hippie-ish idea, but this was a good breakthrough for me. I don't know about you, but it's so easy to get out of bed like a bear with a sore head in the morning, especially if it's early or a gloomy day in the depths of winter. That's when it's natural to think, *Bloody hell, school, exams, work… FML.*

Instead I've learned to take a minute to just chill and to work some positive thoughts into my head. Any minor downers are quickly pushed away, especially if I'm drawing inspiration from the list of categories I call The Marcus Butler Random-Positive-Thought Generator. Give it a go. It might just work for you…

THE RULES:

1. Wake up.
2. Pick three things from the list of categories (below).
3. Spend three minutes thinking about them.
4. Feel happy.
5. Get on with your day.

THE CATEGORIES:

- Things that made me laugh last week
- My greatest achievements
- I'm grateful for…
- Today I'm going to complete these tasks
- Things I'm looking forward to this year…

- My favourite movies
- People I love to death
- My greatest attributes
- Compliments that have made me smile
- The times I've surprised myself

'Here's to the crazy ones. The misfits.
The rebels. The troublemakers.
The round pegs in the square holes.
The ones who see things differently.

They're not fond of rules.

And they have no respect for the status
quo. You can quote them, disagree with
them, glorify or vilify them. About the
only thing you can't do is ignore them.
Because they change things… They push
the human race forward… While some
may see them as the crazy ones, we see
genius. Because the people who are
crazy enough to think they can change
the world, are the ones who do.'

– Steve Jobs, Apple

HOW TO DELIVER A KNOCKOUT PRESENTATION

Public speaking can be terrifying. Every year at school there were debating competitions and everyone had to watch. Whenever I was asked to participate, I always backed out. I'd say,

> 'No way! Public speaking? I struggle to stand up in front of a classroom during presentations, let alone the whole school of 600 people.'

But as I watched the debates, I'd always regret not finding the bravery to get up there. Delivering a killer speech to a big audience looked like a real buzz. Luckily, with my YouTube and business presentations, I've since had a chance to overcome my fears, though there has been a lot of trial and error along the way. Let me walk you through the steps that helped me to success.

1 ▶ GET STUCK IN

Someone's asked you to give a presentation? Try it. Do it in your class. Step up and deliver a speech in your Saturday job or workplace, or even with your sports team. Yeah, it's terrifying: you'll be judged, someone might laugh at you behind your back, but think, *What's the worst that can happen?* Sure, if your flies are undone, or you've tucked your skirt into your knickers, it might be a humiliating experience, but that will pass eventually. Once you've got over the initial fear of public speaking, there's no limit to what you can achieve.

2 ▶ READY YOURSELF

Preparation is key. Unless it's a subject you're so passionate about that you can free talk about it for hours, you'll need to do some prep, especially if it's a school exam or a work pitch. Know your subject inside out, because a question might get thrown at you as the presentation comes to a close. If you haven't prepped, you'll be shown up straight away.

3 ▶ NAIL THAT DELIVERY

Executing your presentation is the death-or-glory moment. Deliver several pages of witty text in a monotone voice and your audience will drift into a coma. Bring energy and smarts to the stage and they'll be hanging off your every word. To perfect your tone, practise a stage voice. Present it to a friend or someone in your family. They'll be honest with you on your delivery. If there's no one around to work on, do it in the mirror.

 **LIFE HACK!**

While watching yourself, consider the importance of body language. Sticking your hands in your pockets can make you look dodgy or unfriendly. But 'steepling' – that's when you put your fingertips together and make a triangle with your hands – can make you look wise, just like the Microsoft boss Bill Gates.

4 ▶ KNOW YOUR AUDIENCE...

I can be myself on camera. If I mess up, people find it funny (well, sometimes), but that doesn't work in serious presentations. I was once flown to Norway to deliver a speech on vlogging to fifty people from high-profile brands. I thought, *Yeah, sure I can do that. I make videos – I can chat to anyone.*

On stage, I tried to be funny, but the crowd didn't laugh and it was awful. I hadn't researched my audience. I thought I had to communicate with them in the same way that I communicated with my viewers, and that was a big mistake. Now I'll never do a presentation without understanding the crowd. Once I've worked out what they're like, I'll alter my delivery accordingly. Oh, quick tip: if you're presenting to teachers, oldies or Norwegian internet executives – no swearing. It's a bit of a buzzkill.

5 ▶ ...THEN KILL IT
(THE PRESENTATION, NOT THEM. THAT WOULD BE WEIRD.)

With steps 1 to 4 completed, the butterflies will kick in as you walk to your stage, but embrace them. Trust yourself. You've prepared, so people are going to listen to your work. Look around the room as you talk; it'll bring the audience into your story. Trust me, you'll be fine. And if the worst comes to the worst, imagine everyone in the audience is naked, on the toilet, constipated. I find that helps to settle my anxiety every time.

HOW TO BREAK A WORLD RECORD

If you want a little example of how being focused and super-positive can help you along in life, then consider this: I've got world records on my CV – nine of them. *Nine.* Sure, several are currently being shared with my mate Alfie, but it's still a pretty impressive haul. To put it into perspective, Usain Bolt only has three for his killer times in the 100 metres, 200 metres and 4 x 100-metre relay, so you can see why I'm pretty proud of the achievement.*

How I came to break those records is a crazy story. First, it happened just as my channel was really taking off. My subscription figures were going through the roof: 20,000, 50,000, 100,000… and people were starting to notice. One day, Guinness World Records reached out and asked if Alfie and I would like to help them in breaking a few established feats for their YouTube channel. We were going to get paid for our efforts, and as part of the deal they intended to film the whole thing – which I'm guessing they thought would be hilarious – while putting us up in a London apartment.

Well, I was pretty excited. For as long as I could remember, I'd been a fan of the *Guinness World Records* book. Mum had bought it for me every Christmas and I must own around fifteen different editions. Every year I'd flick through the

---

* Before we go on, I'm in no way saying I'm to be considered on the same level as The World's Fastest Man. Just in case any of you think I'm getting too cocky. I know that holding the record for 'Most Bangles Put On in Thirty Seconds by a Team of Two' isn't exactly a comparable achievement.

GUINNESS WORLD RECORDS 2015
GUINNESS WORLD RECORDS 2014
GUINNESS WORLD RECORDS 2012
GUINNESS WORLD RECORDS 2011
GUINNESS WORLD RECORDS 2010
GUINNESS WORLD RECORDS 2009
GUINNESS WORLD RECORDS 2008
GUINNESS WORLD RECORDS 2007
GUINNESS WORLD RECORDS 2006
GUINNESS WORLD RECORDS 2005

pages, looking to see who was the world's oldest, tallest and fattest dudes; I loved learning about the weird feats, too, like the person with the longest fingernails. I often wondered what it would take to get my name in there.

Once the idea was put to us, we were hooked. 'Yeah, cool!' we said. 'Let's do it!' Then shortly afterwards the reality of our challenge kicked in. I said to Alfie, 'So what do we do now? What records are we going for? How many scotch eggs can you eat in a minute?' But luckily the people from Guinness World Records had a plan. Well – *ish*.

'So, Alfie, Marcus, we'll come up with a list of easily breakable records,' said their representative. 'In a month we'll see how many of them you can break and we'll film the whole lot.'

It sounded like a lot of fun. Alfie and I packed our bags and headed to London for the first stab at getting our names into the record books – literally. Though we soon discovered that Guinness's challenges were hardly 'easy'. In fact, we sucked at every single one of them. On the first day, for example, they sat us in front of a bowl of hotdogs and asked us to eat more than eight in a minute. I think we only managed three each,

On set filming for Guinness world records with Alfie January 2011

and even that was a proper pain. The last one felt like a brick going into my stomach.

When that failed, somebody suggested that I grip a toothbrush in my teeth while spinning a basketball on the end. 'You played basketball, Marcus,' they said. 'It should be fine.' How wrong could they be? It couldn't have gone any worse! The ball kept tipping off the end, smashing me on the nose as it fell. It was another blown attempt and after a dozen or so failed challenges, I admit it, I started to feel a bit down. I really wanted a world record, but they were all so bloody hard. In the end we decided to make up a few challenges of our own, while breaking some already established records at the same time. And ones that were a lot more manageable than spinning a basketball on the end of a toothbrush gripped between my teeth.

First up was the record for the Highest Number of Hits of a Tennis Ball in One Minute While Using the Alternating Sides of a Racket (unlucky, Andy Murray). Alfie and I then set the Fastest Speed for Making a Sandwich While Blindfolded. Another record was shattered when we managed to lay a table with fine dining cutlery at super-fast speed.

Our proudest moment undoubtedly came when we set the record time for putting bras on one another. We positioned ourselves face to face, ladies' underwear affixed to our manly chests, as we attempted to remove the other's bra as many times as possible in a minute. Boom! We completed six switches and I'm now the world's fastest bra putter-on-er and taker-off-er. Not that I brag about that one too hard in front of Niomi. Or her family for that matter. I'm a world record-breaker, not a knob.

MARCUS'S STEP-BY-STEP GUIDE TO BREAKING A WORLD RECORD

1 ▸ FIND A RECORD THAT'S EASY TO BREAK, OR UTILISE A SKILL OR UNIQUE TALENT

Clearly I'm very good at taking a bra on and off, but you might have a talent in another area, such as stuffing sprouts into your underwear. Call Guinness World Records. Say you want to see how many small vegetables you can get into your pants in one minute and go from there. The more unique the claim, the better. You can submit most suggestions, though they can't be too ludicrous. For example, I remember Alfie and I wanted to set a record for The Fastest Time to Lick an Entire Brick. The adjudicators weren't impressed.

2 ▸ PRACTISE

We didn't break any of those world records without practising. Often we'd get nowhere near a killer time during the early attempts, like with our blindfolded sandwich-making challenge. But if we seemed relatively confident about being successful in the long run, we'd persevere. We'd practise hard. Once our technique was honed, we'd set the cameras rolling…

3 ▸ CONTACT THE EXPERTS

Check out the website and follow their step-by-step guidelines for how to complete and verify a new world record. According to the rule-makers this can be done if you video your attempt and use evidence such as independent witness statements and logbooks, though the process can take a couple of months. But don't stress – it's all explained on the website.

4 ▸ ENJOY SEEING YOUR NAME IN LIGHTS

Once you've shoved a record number of sprouts into your pants, you'll be handed a glass frame, with your name and record engraved on it. It looks great, and it makes for a nice doorstop, but be prepared for challengers. Once word spreads of your success, I guarantee that you'll be asked to recreate the record-breaking accomplishment at every single party you go to. Though strangely no one's challenged me on my bra-unclipping skills yet...

Me and Alfie after smashing the world record for bra-unclipping

THE SUCCESS CONUNDRUM

We all know how to best deal with failure. After a blown exam, disastrous job interview or screwed-up work project, it's best to dust yourself down and get on with life – to try again and not become overly disheartened. It's hard, I know, but all the big hitters in business have experienced disaster in their careers. Look at almost anyone you admire. There are some pretty epic fails in the lives of the super-successful. But what these people rarely do is explain how they've handled success, because, believe me, it can be just as tricky as dealing with failure.

If that sounds weird, let me explain. When I first started out on YouTube I never expected to be a success. I didn't imagine that I would be attracting millions of viewers or bringing out my own book. It came as a shock to me and at times it still feels really surreal. There were moments where I wondered if I deserved it, I had the occasional flashes of self-doubt. Success put me in the public eye and for every ten people that liked me, there was a person or two that didn't. I started getting criticism and nasty comments on my page. It was hard to take at times.

But it's not just in *my* lifestyle where success can be a tricky issue. It can take place in yours, too. Glory can come in the shape of an impressive exam result or job promotion. You might get lauded for some charity work or a spectacular athletic achievement. And when praise comes in from all quarters, it can be hard to handle well. You might not have expected success and the news could go to your head. Handling acclaim might be hard to accept, especially if you're

A Q&A with some of you guys at Vidcon 2014. Live Q&As are one of my favourite things to do - interacting with you, my audience.

a modest person. All of these issues can cause pressure. It can freak people out. But not any more: I'm going to teach you how to handle the ups, and be a better person for it.

IMAGINE SUCCESS: IT COULD BE YOU!

Picture your success at the start of a project, or before you go into a job interview or exam. Of course, you don't want to build yourself up to a point where you could be easily knocked down, so don't get overconfident. And never get ahead of yourself, because you'll only experience disappointment if you fail or fall short. But do imagine how you'd react if your plans come off. That way it won't be a shock if victory comes your way.

PREPARE FOR THE HATERS

The more successful you get in anything, the more people will try to bring you down. Get that job promotion and suddenly you're in a different position. Yeah, it's great news, but there's an added pressure or two to deal with. For example, if you're a newly installed manager, you'll have a team to look after. There are different tasks to do and different characters to care for; there's extra expectation from the people above you. All these things can affect a person, and it's easy to overthink the situation and become thrown off track really quickly.

Then chuck into the mix the fact that you're in a position of power, which you might not have experienced before. You're successful in work, so you'll be made out to be a positive example, and not everyone will like that. Some people might be unhappy that you've become successful. Other people will become jealous. This is going to happen throughout your life, no matter what you're doing – even at school. You're also not going to be able to please everyone, especially if you're telling them what to do.

Girls' night in with Caspar and Alfie. Trying to clear our 'paws' with nose strips

I experienced something similar in my career. The bigger I became on YouTube, the more criticism I got –

as well as the nice stuff – and it did my head in because it was a shock. But if you can tell yourself that it's coming, that some people might get funny about you being successful, then it'll be less of an unpleasant surprise when it happens.

MODESTY

Don't get cocky. I was always brought up to be humble, I was told to be modest in whatever I achieved, and I feel that's very important with success. I'm lucky with my group of mates. The whole YouTube thing hasn't changed our relationship at all. They'll still throw banter my way, which keeps me pretty grounded. Sure, you want to be proud if you're doing well, but you also don't want to be bragging left, right and centre. Don't be the show-off. Don't shove your success down other people's throats.

Having said that, it's important to enjoy your personal achievements. So, think to yourself, *This is great, look at what I've achieved!* Just don't go on about it to the world. You'll only make yourself a bigger target for the haters. And they'll be sure to come for you at the first sign of a slip-up.

REMEMBER, SUCCESS IS A GOOD THING!

Be confident in yourself. Don't think, *I didn't deserve this*, otherwise you'll leave a trail of underlying inferiority. Even if your success was a fortuitous break, chances are you've made that good luck for yourself in some way, so enjoy it.

I remember experiencing this for a while. After I'd won YouTube's Next Up competition I kept thinking, *Wow! Why me? YouTube's a hobby; why have they decided to give this to me? Of course it's massively cool and I feel really appreciative, but am I worthy of it?* Those thoughts kept going through my mind day after day.

I snapped myself out of it when I met the other winners. YouTube had flown everyone to London. They put us all up in a fancy hotel and for a week we worked with Google on a week's training course. In the run-up to the event I was so nervous. I'd convinced myself that everyone else would be way more talented than me. I figured that they would have bigger YouTube channels and larger online followings. But when I met everyone, and realised that we were on the same level, all of that disappeared and those worries went away. I felt a lot more comfortable.

Niomi surprised me with this cake when I found out I had won the YouTube Next Up competition.

SHOW GRATITUDE

Most successful people rarely get to the top on their own; they often get there with the help of someone else – a small favour or a big push. That person might have given them an idea. Someone might have helped them to revise or to train. A teacher, coach or management figure at work could have provided some key expertise on a subject, or an important technique or skill that later proved pivotal to their glory.

If you get that A grade in school and you know your teacher broke their back to help you, then thank them. It's a courtesy thing and it's going to make them feel better. If someone has helped you to become successful, show gratitude. Be thankful for that help.

I wouldn't be where I am today without my viewers. I want to thank them for everything they've done for me. Even if it's just them watching a video of mine or following me on Twitter, that's helped me. Without them I wouldn't be doing this – I'd be nothing – and I don't know where I'd be working. I'd probably still be at uni, or chasing down some business idea. I certainly wouldn't be leading the life I am now.

EVERYONE SEES SUCCESS DIFFERENTLY

What one individual might see as success, another might see as insignificant. If you're a person who views the things you do as a great achievement, that's amazing, but don't compare your work to someone else's. Other people's achievements shouldn't be considered as bigger than yours or inferior. (No one likes a bully, remember?) So if you've just made your first short movie, don't go moaning because it doesn't live up to the latest Steven Spielberg masterpiece.

Be proud of what you've done and where you're going. If you constantly knock yourself down, you're never going to believe in your own successes. Start criticising your achievements, or comparing them to others, and you'll diminish your satisfaction. You don't deserve to feel crap. You're a winner, remember!

So here we are at the end of the book. It could be that you've read the whole thing from cover to cover, maybe you've flicked through and picked out the sections that are relevant to you, or maybe you just stared at the pictures (that's what I'd probably do first!). Either way, I hope you've enjoyed it and that maybe one day it will come in useful.

I know from my own experiences that life isn't always easy – it can give you a kick when you least expect it, and it often brings problems that can't be solved in 24 hours. But with some of the advice you've picked up here, and a little help from your mates and loved ones, those challenges – hopefully – won't seem too tough to overcome.

Thank you to each and every one of you reading this right now for making the last five years so unbelievably incredible for me, and of course for buying my book! Your continued support for everything I do is more than I could ask for and I would be truly lost without you guys. I'd love to know what you think of the book. I can't wait to hopefully meet you in person and discuss. :)

Marcus x

CURE THE HICCUPS

Everyone has their theory on how to cure the hiccups, but I find that drinking a glass of water upside down usually does the trick. If this sounds crazy, the next time you have a fit, place your mouth over the opposite side of a glass of water and tip backwards. Begin sipping and – bang! – your hiccups are cured! You'll have to turn your head a little, and you'll definitely get some funny looks because you'll spill a lot, but it works. Don't do it in a fancy restaurant unless you want to get kicked out.

THE IPHONE CRADLE

You're on a train and you want to watch something on your phone (one of my videos, maybe?) but you don't have one of those fancy cases. Annoying, right? Well, get your sunglasses or glasses and rest the phone in the folded arms. It works perfectly as a makeshift TV stand and is great for when you go travelling.

ACKNOWLEDGEMENTS

This is the section of the book where I'm meant to leave thanks and all that for the people who actually made this book possible. (Warning: don't expect some kind of A-class Oscar acceptance speech).

Firstly my thanks have to go to you: my viewers. As I've said many times before, I truly appreciate every single one of you for continuously supporting me. Thank you for taking the time to read my book.

Sarah Emsley and Holly Harris from Headline Publishing, who basically made this book possible from start to finish.

Matt Allen for the countless hours we spent together working on the text in the book. My words wouldn't have made much sense without his help.

Niomi, for her constant love and support in everything I do. The same to my family: Mum, Dad, stepdad Simon and sisters Tash and Heidi.

The people I work with closely at Gleam: Lucy, who holds everything together and helps me make important decisions; Alex and Chloe for making my day to day life a little easier; and to Dom for helping to make things possible.

All of my YouTube friends for sharing the same passions and ambitions in this crazy amazing YouTube world we're in.

My best mates from back home, for keeping me grounded and always being there for a laugh.

And to Jermayne, who, by inspiring me to change my lifestyle, helped to inspire this book.

THE END :-)